CHECK POINTS ON
HOW TO BUY
ORIENTAL RUGS

CHECK POINTS ON

HOW TO BUY
ORIENTAL RUGS

CHARLES W. JACOBSEN

CHARLES E. TUTTLE COMPANY: PUBLISHERS

Rutland, Vermont   Tokyo, Japan

Representatives
Continental Europe: BOXERBOOKS, INC., Zurich
British Isles: PRENTICE-HALL INTERNATIONAL, INC., London
Australasia: PAUL FLESCH & CO., PTY. LTD., Melbourne
Canada: M. G. HURTIG LTD., Edmonton

Published by the Charles E. Tuttle Company, Inc.
of Rutland, Vermont & Tokyo, Japan
with editorial offices at
Suido 1-chome, 2–6, Bunkyo-ku, Tokyo, Japan

Library of Congress Catalog Card No. 73–94020
Standard Book No. 8048-0714-0

PRINTED IN JAPAN

TABLE OF CONTENTS

ILLUSTRATIONS

FIGURES

PLATES

The black-and-white plates, for the most part, illustrate rare rugs that are collector's items which, naturally, are of the most interest. Even when worn thin they are desirable, but one must remember that the better the condition, the more valuable they are. Defects, except for crookedness in shape and bad changes of color, unfortunately, are not easily discernible in black-and-white prints.

PREFACE

In the preface of my large book, *Oriental Rugs—A Complete Guide*, published by The Charles E. Tuttle Company, Inc., Tokyo, Japan & Rutland, Vermont, a volume of 479 pages, I said, "I know that as I write I will have to delete and omit many discussions that I would like to present." This, because of the size of the book.

The sale of this book, the world over, has exceeded all expectations. It has been reprinted many times.

The thousands of letters received regarding it have, without exception, been complimentary.

It is our belief that more copies have been distributed in the United States than the combined total of all other books on the subject during the past fifty years.

The hundreds of letters requesting information have induced me to write now in considerable detail on the subject, "How to Buy Oriental Rugs." "How to Keep From Getting Gyped in Buying Oriental Rugs" was suggested for a talk to the Women's Club of Naples, Florida, where we have our winter home.

My previous book did give some sound advice for the rug purchaser in Chapter Twenty-Three. The many letters I receive daily from people seeking information, tells me that I need to devote an entire volume to this subject. It is my hope that the detailed discussions under the several check points will save me much letter writing.

Even here in Florida, during my winter vacation, it is necessary that I employ a full-time secretary just to answer these requests. These are in addition to the heavy mail that our corporation receives in Syracuse concerning the purchase of rugs.

This new book will include a chapter on the changes that have occurred during the past eight years, and also important information on the "Future Outlook," which is quite dim at the moment. Also, we are including a chapter on the "Care of Oriental Rugs," with special emphasis on the care and cleaning of your rugs in your own home.

I make no acknowledgment for help in preparing this book. It is based on my 46 years in the business, during which time I probably have bought more oriental rugs than any other active retail oriental rug buyer. If I owe anyone thanks for help it will be the many importers in New York and my buyers abroad. We have discussed the many problems together many times.

The only real acknowledgment for help in preparing this book is due my dear wife, Virginia, in proofreading, and to my secretary, Miss Josephine D'Agostino, who made many good corrections and contributions.

My staff and I have for many years practiced the procedure we have suggested for you to follow.

Chapter One

INTRODUCTION

The layman or buyer of his first oriental rug may well wonder, and may well ask, why one would have to check so carefully in purchasing a NEW Oriental rug.

Why isn't a new oriental rug perfect?

Why should one need to use this check list to buy a completely new rug and especially if one buys it from some well-known store?

The sad fact is that a good percentage of the new rugs coming from Iran will have faults and defects that cause us and many other dealers to reject them.

The rugs that require the least inspection by our check list are the orientals coming to America from India. They have 100% wool nap and the tag must indicate if other materials are used. Later we will cover certain faults to look for in these.

The Bokhara rugs from West Pakistan are coming with very few faults. You do have to watch out for a few of them being quite crooked in shape, and for a small number being clipped too short (low nap). Also, there is some bad clipping (different height of nap) on some few of the excellent Karachi quality Bokharas.

The rugs from Afghanistan will need the same checking as the rugs from Iran.

AT NO TIME IN THE PAST 75 YEARS HAVE THE ODDS BEEN SO AGAINST THE LAYMAN OR NOVICE, OR BUYER OF HIS FIRST ORIENTAL RUG.

AT NO TIME IN HISTORY HAS THE MERCHANDISING AND ADVERTISING OF ORIENTAL RUGS REACHED SUCH A LOW UNETHICAL LEVEL BY MANY LARGE STORES.

This is not to condemn the many fine dealers to be found over the country, but with so many well-known stores employing the "USED RUG SALE" gimmick as their principal means of selling oriental rugs,

HOW IS THE PUBLIC TO KNOW which is a reliable store for buying oriental rugs?

The "USED RUG SALE" vehicle was originally used by New York stores. But lately, this method has been adopted by many of the best known stores around the country. Most of these, outside the large cities in the East, do not have a regular oriental rug department, and let outsiders bring in their used rugs for the special, once or twice a year, sales.

I go into this in great detail in my chapter on "Used Rug Sales" to try to guide you to one of the oriental rug dealers who does not run these unethical and highly exaggerated used rug ads.

AT NO TIME IN HISTORY HAVE SO MANY NEW RUGS, IMPORTED FROM IRAN, REACHED SUCH A LOW LEVEL OF QUALITY IN GENERAL. This statement applies more specifically to the thousands of rugs in many different types being woven in the great Hamadan District. As you read this book in its entirety you will come to the conclusion that it is a difficult situation, and, instead of being corrected, will likely get worse. Be sure and read Chapter Nine on "Outlook for the Future on Oriental Rugs."

I rather suspect that the dealers in Iran, and the importers in America, will not make an effort to correct or improve the situation, but rather they will try to find rugs at a price at which they will be salable in America. The steps being taken by the Iranian Government in the past few weeks and those indicated for the future, will, in our opinion, mean higher prices at once and sizable increases each year, and perhaps, within the next five, or ten years at most, the end of weaving of oriental rugs to a large extent in Iran.

There are still very wonderful rugs being woven in Iran today, but it requires careful screening and searching out for the best ones. And you should heed my TWO MOST IMPORTANT ADMONITIONS: *FIRST*, "Never buy an oriental rug at an AUCTION SALE (itinerant auction)" and *SECOND*, "Be very cautious in buying an oriental rug, new or used, at a USED RUG SALE."

Then, here is a check list that can help you when buying your first rugs. It can help the dealer and collector and, I might add, it will help me and my assistants if we used this check list ourselves.

As I have already stated, one of the main reasons for presenting this book is to have something in print that will answer and cover many of the questions that come to me daily from people all over the world.

The thousands of letters from collectors, dealers, and individuals,

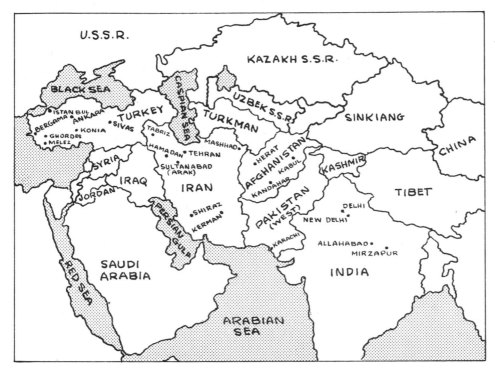

Figure 1. Map showing important rug-weaving areas.

who have purchased my large book, *Oriental Rugs—A Complete Guide,* have, without exception, been complimentary. To be sure some few of the used rug dealers, and some of those dealers who over the years sold mostly the "chemically washed and painted variety of oriental rugs," could not have applauded, but they were good enough not to tell or write me.

Where does the blame lie for so many of the new orientals coming in having such bad faults? I am sure that many of the defects in the thousands of Hamadan types are due to the fact that practically all of the grown men and women in this district, especially in the large city of Hamadan, have quit weaving and have gone to work in the new factories at higher salaries. This has left the older people and the children, to a large extent, to do the weaving. The fault also lies with the factors who seek to turn out certain name and type rugs for less. Much of it is due to the carelessness in clipping by small children.

Over the years I have talked to many buyers for the different importing houses and urged them to be more selective. In the past I have been able to buy abroad under nearly the same conditions as they buy, and in a large group of rugs in one importation, will find only a few of them with objectionable defects. I don't go on buying trips to Iran any more, but we do have a buyer who is very careful in his buying in Iran, and we come up with very few rugs with bad faults. True, we pay a little more. It is very difficult to get selection at a good price in Iran, especially in buying the small rugs, runners, and rugs up to 9×12 ft.

The last people I would want to hurt, in calling attention to the many miserable rugs from this district, are the many importers who have been my good friends over the past 46 years. These importers are very reliable and they do not try to "put one over" on the stores who buy their leftover rugs. They will take back any rug a retailer may wish to return after it arrives in the retailer's store.

Nor do I blame too much the scores of small jobbers of used rugs who, in most cases, will do the cheapest job possible to make a badly worn rug presentable. I refer principally to the touching up of worn out places, and the touching up of moth-eaten places, on the underside of the rug to cover where the damage is. OF COURSE, THIS IS ONE OF THE DOWNRIGHT CROOKED PRACTICES USED. But, here again, these small jobbers have the operators and buyers of these "USED RUG SALES" come to them for this lowest price type of rug.

I think that the blame lies chiefly on the merchandise managers of these large stores, and their oriental rug buyers. Of course, I am referring to the "Used Rug Sales."

Perhaps some of my friends in the trade will accuse me of setting my own yardstick. Anyone who reads this book in its entirety cannot fail to note that I have not prescribed a narrow-minded point of view. I have always agreed that the handmade oriental rug cannot be as perfect as a machine made rug. If they were, they would lose much of their charm. We are warning against the serious and objectionable faults.

It is hoped to make you realize, first as well as last, the indisputable fact that you cannot now secure desirable oriental rugs for a song, and it is safe to rest assured generally that he who sells an oriental rug very cheap, is selling a very cheap oriental rug as well.

Plates 1 & 2. SAVONNERIE rugs in home of Colonel Jacobsen, Naples, Florida. Design 9612–B, ivory with border in two shades of green and two of light blue, and field of light sand beige. Similar to Plate 1 in our large book (design 9612–C) but without the medallion in the field. Also made with a field of soft gold, soft green, white, or rose. These plates show the simplicity and the beauty of these rugs and also point up an item on the "Care of Oriental Rugs" discussed in Chapter Eleven. Both rugs have been in use for eight years. The living room rug is still in like-new condition and only recently has been sponged off. The dining room rug has been sponged every few months. Though used only six months of the year, they prove their superiority over wall-to-wall carpeting in regard to ease of care, and durability. Many of our friends have replaced their wall-to-wall carpeting during this same period.

Plate 3. KHYBER from India, in green and white. Also comes in golden buff and white, light blue and white, and lemon yellow and white. Comes in all Standard sizes from 2×3 feet to 12×20 feet.

Plate 4. KEEN-LUNG with Chinese design, from India, in creamy ivory and blue. Also made with several different shades of gold or green replacing the blue, and in other colors as well. Sold under various trade names by different importers. KEEN-LUNG is the exclusive trade name of Charles W. Jacobsen, Inc. Made in all standard sizes up to 12×20 feet.

Plate 5. CASTILE with Spanish design, from India, in gold with ivory background. Also made with blue, green, or navy replacing the gold. Benares indicates the producer's quality. Comes in all standard sizes up to 12×20 feet.

Chapter Two

CHECK POINTS FOR BUYING A NEW ORIENTAL RUG

EACH POINT LISTED IS COVERED IN DETAIL IN CHAPTER SIX

1. IS THE RUG VERY IRREGULAR IN SHAPE? TOO CROOKED? Slight irregularities in oriental rugs are to be expected; very crooked rugs are objectionable.

2. CHANGES OF COLOR. Slight shadings and changes of color are to be expected. Radical changes are usually objectionable.

3. DOES THE RUG LIE FLAT? Insist on rug being flat. Wrinkles sized out, but make sure the dealer sizes the rug. Don't let anyone tell you the wrinkles will walk out with use.

4. EDGES CURLED UNDER ON MANY TIGHTLY WOVEN RUGS. A serious but correctable fault. Don't accept rug until correction is made.

5. IS THE RUG BADLY CLIPPED? Does rug have a thick nap in one area and very thin nap in other areas? Reduces rug salability.

6. LOOSE OR BLEEDING COLORS. Red or blue discoloring white area is usually objectionable to most people. Bad stains reduce values. Most can be bleached out.

7. POORLY OVERCAST SIDES AND ENDS NOT PROPERLY SECURED. Vast majority of new Persians are not properly finished. Easily corrected, but most retailers do nothing about this. Importers do nothing on these.

The beginner can easily check on the above seven points. The next four check points are not easily discernible, and you have to rely on the dealer to protect you on these points. Remember the advice, "Buy from a reliable store where you can return the rug for credit if necessary."

8.   CHEMICALLY WASHED AND PAINTED RUGS. Not a real problem today! (Except on used rugs.) Only rugs so treated are a small percentage of Sarouks and a very few Dergazine runners. We never liked these washed and painted rugs but many dealers would still sell these if available. The dealer will probably tell you, if you asked, whether the rug is chemically washed or not.

9.   SALTWATER DAMAGE. Little danger of this in a good store; yet a possibility, especially at auctions. Read detailed discussion.

10.   JUFTI KNOT. You cannot do anything about this point. Only indicates rug is less compact. Majority of Persian rugs cheat some with Jufti knot. Many fine types have not resorted to this.

11.   DEAD WOOL. It is just about the worse fault that can occur in a new rug. Wool removed from butchered sheep with lye. Wool is brittle and wears down in two or three years, instead of forty. Reliable dealer is the answer. Read detailed discussion.

12.   ORIENTAL RUGS FROM INDIA. Require very little checking for faults. Many qualities easily compared for prices. Tag must show composition of nap, i.e., 100% wool, or 70% wool, 30% jute. Very few without 100% wool nap.

13.   PRICES. Cannot be of much help here. A little common sense is all that is necessary. Read detailed discussion.

14.   IS THE RUG A REAL HANDMADE ORIENTAL RUG? Federal Trade Commission requires that advertisement says "Oriental Design" and not "Oriental Rugs." Nevertheless, many stores including some big ones run misleading ads. The machine-made rug has more of a stamped-out look.

Chapter Three

CHECK POINTS FOR BUYING
A USED ORIENTAL RUG

EACH POINT LISTED IS COVERED IN
DETAIL IN CHAPTER SEVEN

Used includes antiques, semi-antiques, and used orientals of every type.

Buying a used rug at an auction of an itinerant auctioneer or dealer is the greatest risk of all. But whether buying at a "Used Rug Sale" in a store or private sale in a home, or auction of contents of a home or estate, you will do well to check the rug against this check list.

1. WHAT IS THE CONDITION OF THE RUG?
    a. Does it have a good nap?
    b. Is it slightly thin?
    c. Is it badly worn or threadbare?
    d. Has the background been touched up with dye or ink to conceal worn-out places?

A badly worn rug may be worth one-tenth or less than the same rug in good condition. You must get right down on the rug and examine it with your hands. Discovering the condition in one of the above categories is not difficult, even for the layman.

2. EXAMINE SIDES AND ENDS. They can be refinished, but it oftentimes costs more than the old rug is worth.
    a. Do sides require new overcasting?
    b. Are ends loose and is a part of border or corners already missing?
    c. Are edges curled under?
Only cutting part of borders will correct these faults.

3.   HAS RUG HAD CONSIDERABLE REPAIR? A small amount of good repair work hurts a rug very little. Badly repaired places that will need opening up and re-weaving or patching reduce the value greatly. Repair may be prohibitive.

4.   HAS RUG BEEN CUT? If reduced in size to make the rug shorter or smaller, or to eliminate a damaged area, it is generally worth about one-half after being cut and sewed together.

5.   MOTH DAMAGE OR HOLES IN RUG. One of the most important check points. Small moth damage can be repaired. Extensive damage to nap, sides, and especially on underside where knots are cut and can readily be pulled out from the nap side, reduces the value greatly; often reduces values from $500.00 to $50.00, or even to no value.

6.   IS IT A CHEMICALLY WASHED AND PAINTED RUG? A used rug of any type so treated has much less value than an antique or natural-colored rug of the same type. Never becomes antique or semi-antique. Used rug sales have many of this type.

7.   HAIRBRUSHES AND CHANGES OF COLOR. Slight change is to be expected in most all antiques and semi-antiques and is not objectionable. Radical changes that detract from the beauty do lower the value, but not as much as with a new rug.

8.   STRAIGHT OR CROOKED? More irregularity in shape in old rugs is to be expected. Very crooked rugs are still objectionable.

9.   DOES RUG LIE FLAT OR ARE THERE CONFIRMED WRINKLES? No rug should be used on the floor unless it lies flat. Old rugs, when allowed to wrinkle for years (confirmed wrinkles), can only be sized flat with difficulty and cutting is usually the only correction.

10.   LOOSE OR BLEEDING COLORS. Appear on ivory nap. Hurts value of old rug more than a new one.

11.   DRY ROT OR SALTWATER DAMAGE. Old rugs that have laid on ground floors in Iran often become tender in places and weak in some spots. Same as saltwater damage. Rug has very little value.

Plates 6 and 7. This rug and the one on the next page were both once rare and choice CABISTANS from Caucasia, but now are poor buys at $10.00 each. The one above can be salvaged for a few years' use by taking off the border and refinishing it, but it will still be thin and of little value. The one on the next page is completely worn out and could not be repaired for $100.00. Its only value is for use as patches in repairing other rugs.

Plate 7. Caption on preceding page.

12. JUFTI KNOT. Very few old rugs will have this as a rule. Only those woven since 1945. You can't eliminate them and the rug is just somewhat more loosely woven. And it does not ruin the rug.

13. WHITE KNOTS IN RUG. When white knots show it usually means the rug is worn down to the warp. See detailed discussion. Be most careful on old Chinese rugs with white knots and where they have been touched up. See No. 16 below on old Chinese rugs.

14. SPOTS ON RUG. Small depressed burns and ink spots are usually to be found on old rugs from Iran. Easily corrected. Sizable BAD SPOTS are objectionable and reduce value greatly.

15. GLUE, LASTEX, OR NON-SKID SUBSTANCE ON BACK OF RUG. A quick look at underside of rug shows this. Resale value reduced to less than half.

16. CHINESE RUGS. A real danger point. Check thinness, white knots, and stains. One 9×12 may be worth $25.00 to $50.00; another one $500.00.

17. USED RUGS FROM INDIA. Those made since World War II. Check mainly for bad spots on these light backgrounds.

18. IS RUG A REAL ORIENTAL OR A MACHINE-MADE COPY? See check point No. 14 in Chapter Two on new rugs. The machine-made rug has a stamped-out regularity. Place it beside a real oriental and the difference is apparent.

19 PRICES. Unless you are buying an inexpensive rug get some help. No way to eliminate element of gamble in a short time. If you read and study our detailed discussion on this subject in this book, you will find considerable help.

Plate 8. NAIN from Iran. This finest of fine rugs has approximately 600 knots to the square inch, which makes it finer than most rugs ever woven. Will seldom have any of the fourteen faults listed in Chapter Six. They never contain any jufti knots and are seldom irregular in shape or have radical changes of color. They are about as perfect as hand-woven rugs can be made. Most of them are about the size of this rug, 8 × 5.5 feet, though some few are smaller or larger.

Plate 9, above. RED SARABEND SAROUK from Iran. One of the best quality Sarouks ever produced, using the old Sarabend design. Will seldom have any of the faults listed in Chapter Six except for minor irregularities described in check points 1, 2, 3, and 4, but not in 5 and most of the others. Size 9×12 feet. *Plate 10, below.* SARABEND SAROUK from Iran. This Sarouk has all the same qualities as that shown in Plate 9. Size 9×12 feet.

Plate 11, above. MISHKIN from Northern Iran. This thick oriental uses the old Caucasian Kazak design and is reasonable in price, being, perhaps, a better investment as floor covering than the very scarce and expensive old Caucasian rugs, particularly the antique Kazak. A number of people have paid the old Caucasian price for these rugs at auctions. Size 7 × 11 feet. Plate 12, below. Some as Plate 11. Size 7.3 by 10.1 feet.

LN-1029

Plate 13, above. PRAYER rug from Pakistan, using the design of the famous old Mondjour family prayer rug in the Turkish Museum. Its new name in Pakistan is Saph. It is finely woven and usually has three prayer designs in different colors, but occasionally it has seven, each in a different color. To date all are in runner sizes. Used frequently as tapestry, but durable enough for any floor use. Size 6 × 3 feet. *Plate 14, below*. BOKHARA from West Pakistan. The old name was Tekke or Royal Bokhara, and the present name in Pakistan is Mori. It comes in two qualities, the LaHore and the heavier Karachi, with variations in both qualities. Nearly half of the Karachi quality are woven with an ivory background. Many used rug sales list these new Bokharas as "condition excellent," giving the impression they are used Bokharas in excellent condition, or at least hoping the public will think so.

Chapter Four

AUCTIONS

The greatest gamble of all in buying an oriental rug is to buy it at an auction.

This was true fifty years ago and it is true today. I have no interest in trying to alarm the auction addict into not buying an oriental rug at auction, because he or she is going to said auction in the hope of getting something for less than what it is worth. This is not 100 percent true, but it is generally the case with oriental rugs. An auction of an estate of which you have personal knowledge is a different thing.

THE ITINERANT AUCTIONEER

It is of the itinerant oriental rug auctions that I write. A person here hasn't as much chance as one who goes to the gambling casino or plays the slot machine, because here one might win one or more rounds and if one has sense enough to quit while he is ahead, that is one thing.

But at the oriental rug auction he hasn't that chance. As a rule, the rug is not going to be sold until the bidding has reached a certain price, namely, the price at which the auctioneer owns the rug plus a profit (but more often has it on consignment from some dealer in New York, or elsewhere). That certain price will be his cost plus, as a rule, at least 20 percent, which will barely give him an even break. The motel or place of auction will take a certain percentage of the sales, or he has to pay a few hundred dollars rental for the one or two days sale.

Always there are shills (their own hired people, their own bidders) to bid the rug in at a price that will not be less than the cost and expenses. Never forget, he has to bring one or more trucks to the motel, he has to bring several people with him, and he has paid handsomely for advertising in the papers.

YOU MAY BE SURE THAT HIS OVERHEAD IS MORE

THAN THAT OF YOUR LOCAL DEALER'S. In other words, your local dealer can sell you a rug for *less than he can, and a better one.*

It is safe to surmise and actually say that he cannot hope to come out ahead unless he can get you to bid at least $150.00 for a rug that cost him $100.00, or $1500.00 for a rug he has on consignment for $1000.00. Too often he gets much more.

We will go back to some of these details later in this discussion.

And always, you have to remember that the chances of getting a first quality rug of the different types is small, and that more often the rugs offered are those which have been rejected by many retail dealers in the wholesale market. That is the principal reason why the importing houses are willing to give them to these auctioneers on consignment while retaining title.

These auctioneers with headquarters in some one city, go from city to city holding these auctions for one or two days. They hold them at motels, and any place with a seating capacity, near the city. In my own city there is an ordinance that keeps them out of Syracuse or from operating inside the city limits, but they get by this by going to a motel outside the city limits.

It is this type of auction that is the main target of my criticism. We will give you a few concrete examples of what you can expect at such auctions.

I am not advising you against some auctions, such as the great auction house in New York City, which handles some of the finest estates and art collections in the world. Nor am I advising you to buy a rug there, because more than at any place you need to be an expert or have a real expert adviser to bid on any of the rare rugs that might be offered at the prices they will bring. I do not mean to imply that all of the rugs they offer are rare rugs.

PERMANENT AUCTION HOUSES

There are many permanent auction houses in different cities over the country and they do, from time to time, get well-known estates. My advice is that you can do better at a reliable store, or at least not gamble as heavily.

Now, everybody likes to go to the auctions in private homes, and it can be fun if you are buying small articles or if you know what you are buying. Unfortunately, at many of these sales, outside rugs are brought in to swell the offerings and profit for the auctioneer.

If you are a friend of the family and know the rugs they had in the

Figure 2. The biggest gamble in buying an oriental rug is buying from the itinerant auctioneer. Seldom is a rug sold until it reaches a profitable point. Their own bidders, better known as shills, see to this.

home, then these are the rugs to bid on. But, at the same time, make a careful examination of the different check-list points. Examine for thinness, repairs, especially moth damage on the back, and condition of edges and ends.

Again, the poorest place and greatest risk of all is buying at the itinerant auctioneer's sale.

AUTHORITIES AND WRITERS HAVE WARNED
AGAINST BUYING AT AUCTIONS

I could quote pages of advice by experts from time immemorial who warned against this type of thing.

Mr. A. U. Dilley, in his first little book published in 1909 on page 12 warned against auctions, and I quote:

"At the ordinary rug auction, extravagant and false statement is at its height, and generally the bids are as fictitious as the merits of the rugs are overestimated. The rugs are consigned largely by wholesalers who wish to dispose of the leftover portion of a shipment, or by firms which practice the purchase of cheap rugs with possibilities. These rugs undergo every process of conversion, become the rarest of antiques, and are sold only when the bids advance to a satisfactory figure."

That was said sixty years ago, and the exact words will stand true today. Break down this very accurate statement of Dilley's, and it is as true today as it was in 1909.

When he says the bids are fictitious, and adds "and are sold only when the bids advance to a satisfactory figure," he means that shills (persons allied or employed by the auctioneer) put in many bids, and bid the rug up until it reaches a satisfactory figure. If the rug cost him $100.00 and he has 25 percent overhead for rent, advertising, employees who accompany him, etc., these shills will bid until it reaches $150.00. If the bids don't go that high, then by having it bid in by one of his men keeps him from losing. That is what Dilley meant by the bids being fictitious.

Actually, many clever auctioneers pick bids right out of the air, until the bid gets to the right price or a profitable one. Then, when one unsuspecting person sticks in one bid, little realizing theirs is the only honest bid that has been made, he is declared the purchaser.

The above may not be the general case, but it has happened many times.

Dilley says, "as fictitious as the merits of the rugs are overestimated." If you have attended one of these auctions, you must have wondered at some of the auctioneer's statements. We have had reliable representatives (members of our staff) at these auctions who know rugs—who have heard exaggerations such as, when referring to a medium quality Kirman, 10×14 ft., with a retail value from $1300.00 to $1600.00, announcing, "This is a $4000.00 value,"—or words to that effect.

Recently, the *American Home Magazine* printed an article on "How to Buy an Oriental Rug"—and I quote—

"It is not advisable if you are inexperienced with oriental rugs to pick up something at auctions."

MANY ARE THE REJECTS OR LEFTOVERS

Where do these rugs come from which the itinerant auctioneer offers you with some ridiculous story as to why they must be sacrificed? Actually, many, if not most, of them are what Mr. Dilley calls leftovers. Leftovers, or rejects, is a good description of these rugs.

Every retail dealer in America, as well as every importer, knows that a good percentage of the rugs arriving at their showrooms are hard to sell and have defects easily discernible. Some are less beautiful or, shall we say, approach ugliness.

Why would the importer buy them? We could write a book on the buying of rugs today.

The Iranian rugs are assembled by dealers in Iran in groups according to size and types. Today one goes to Teheran and does not have to travel to the several great rug weaving centers of Hamadan, Meshed, Kirman, Arak, Tabriz, and the smaller centers of Kashan, Gum, Shiraz, and others. They are assembled in Teheran.

The importer must, as a rule, buy groups. He can seldom select from a group, and especially when they have to compete with German and other European buyers, who truly buy with abandon. The American dealer would go broke if he bought the groups the Germans buy, but he does have to buy groups in Iran in sizes to include 9 × 12 ft. rugs.

And every single importer in the New York market accumulates and has to work off these poorer or hard to sell rugs (I call them dogs, or rejects). He has ways to dispose of them.

One means of disposal of these rugs is the used rug sale. The large stores conducting these promotions include many new rugs. Often most of the rugs offered are new. See our discussion of this under Chapter Five, "USED RUG SALES."

Next, the auction houses, and especially the itinerant auctioneer, either buy these leftover rugs at a low price, or, as is more often the case, take them on consignment. This is not to say that every rug these itinerant auctioneers offer is a reject.

Also, a number of drifters get rugs on consignment and put on sales in large stores that do not carry oriental rugs. Generally, they are there a week or ten days. They often have one of the finer Nains, Goums, etc. But if you will compare one he offers to one you find at your regular dealer, or in a reliable store, you will note that even though it is a very fine rug, like the Nain, when placed beside one in a good store, it is lacking, or not nearly so beautiful.

I have noted these itinerant sales this winter in a number of southern cities. A Nain that we sell for $1100.00 to $1300.00 would be listed (in the same size) as regular price, $4000.00; sale price, $2000.00. I have copies of ads from these itinerant sales, often being held in stores of good reputation, with some of the most ridiculous pricing.

For example, a 10 × 14 ft. Bokhara from Pakistan—listed as regular

37

price, $4000.00; sale price, $2000.00. Assuming it to be one of the best of the excellent Karachi quality Bokharas from Pakistan, a good price would be $1200.00, to a very maximum of $1400.00. And we have many fine Bokharas in the LaHore quality that we sell for $550.00 to $850.00 in this size. (In years to come this mentioning of prices will be a mistake on my part.)

SOME TRAGIC CASES

It would take pages to detail the many tragic purchases at such auctions of which we have personal knowledge and data. Indeed, it would be painful to list the many cases of regretful purchases at auctions which have come to our attention. So, we will give just a few typical cases.

The gentleman from Canada, spending the night at a motel near Syracuse where the auction was held that evening, paid $750.00 for an approximate 9×12 ft. LaHore Bokhara from Pakistan, and discovered the next day a number of small holes in the rug. Our repair department charged him $100.00 for repairs. He could have bought a better and perfect rug, same type Bokhara, from us for $550.00. Many Bokharas cost more, but this was average to poor LaHore quality, and not one of the best of Pakistan Bokharas.

Then, the lady in Syracuse who has a dress shop wanted us to buy a runner from her. When it was brought to our store, we found it so very crooked that it could not lay in any hall, nor could it be used on a staircase. In fact, no operation whatsoever, either by cutting out sections, or by sizing, could make it acceptable. It was one of the most irregular runners we have seen. She informed me that she had bought it from a certain auction in a motel near Syracuse, and had actually paid either $225.00 or $325.00 for it (it slips my memory but it was one or the other figure, and I believe she said $325.00). The runner was not salable at any price. She could have bought an excellent runner of same name and size for much less.

There come to mind so many similar cases, and while I do not wish to bore you with many of these, I must give you one or two more on these itinerant auction sales, which are so typical of many cases that have come to our attention.

A lady living in the Westvale section of Syracuse was out for a ride with her sister on Sunday afternoon and saw the auction in progress at the motel. According to her, she had no idea of buying a rug, and with so many bids she did not think she wou'd get the rug if she made one bid. She was surprised when she had the rug for her $850.00 bid.

Early the next morning she came to our store and wanted to know if we had a certain name 9 × 12 ft. rug from India. I was called in and told her we had the rug in the same size for $450.00. I remarked that two of our salesmen who observed the auction reported a lady paid $850.00 for the exact same rug.

She quickly confessed she was the one and that she had already stopped payment on her check before she came to see us. She remarked that her husband would be furious if he knew she had bought a rug.

The rug she bought was a real oriental imported by a firm at 245 Fifth Avenue, New York City, who uses his own trade name for this rug; it has a certain design that comes in three or four background colors. No other importer infringes on his trade name, and the wholesale price is about $300.00. So, there was no question of the auctioneer's rug at $850.00, and my rug at $450.00 being one and the same kind.

The lady assured us hat she and her husband would come in and buy a rug from us in a few days. We never heard from her since that day.

So, you see why I say that most people who attend an oriental rug auction seldom go to a good store, but go to an auction thinking they will get a great bargain.

I repeat, these orientals from India, with the different trade names, indicate a definite quality and design from a certain company in India. There are many companies, each with different trade names.

This is not true of Persian rugs, as each rug of the same name will vary in some degree in design, weave, quality, and beauty. The one exception to this is the contract quality (best) Kirman which is made from paper scale models, and where all the wool is on hand for the rug and the company uses the exact dyes for the rug employing a certain paper scale design.

So much for the itinerant auctioneer, who comes to the vicinity of those cities where oriental rugs have been made popular by good dealers over the years. This man, who comes to our vicinity, comes from a city where oriental rugs have not been made as popular as they are in Syracuse. I can tell you one specific reason why they are not as popular; that is because that large town was offered too many chemically washed and painted oriental rugs over the past 48 years. Everyone in the trade knows which towns used to favor these. Three towns that seldom offered them were my own town of Syracuse, Rochester, and Boston.

People who have owned chemically washed and painted orientals, regardless of how finely woven and how expensive they were, never become real rug enthusiasts or collectors.

I am sure that up until twelve years ago, when the process was practically discontinued (see my discussion on the "Chemically Washed and Painted Rug"), more than half the rugs sold in his town, and the percentage was no doubt much larger, were chemically washed and painted.

Now, this auctioneer who comes to our vicinity has his place in a city some four times as large as Syracuse. We happen to know that he buys only a fraction of the amount of orientals that we buy, including rugs for his auction sales over the country. I believe that if you discount his auctions in towns outside his own city, that we in Syracuse, a city one-fourth as large as his, sell twenty times as many oriental rugs.

So, we could write a book on the itinerant auctioneer. It is here that you run the greatest risk of all in being gypped or badly misled in buying an oriental rug.

KIRMAN FROM ATLANTIC CITY AUCTION

I must write just one more case that came to my attention a few years ago. I think of this because only the other day I had a letter from this gentleman, asking for an appraisal for insurance purposes, of a rug he purchased from us, and he added that they loved their rug more than ever.

This prominent clothing manufacturer, whom we will call Mr. E., and his wife, while at Atlantic City, bought a Kirman carpet approximately 10×14 ft. at auction, paying $2000.00 for the rug.

When this rug arrived he telephoned me (since I lived only three or four blocks from him) and asked me to come over and help him in his claim against the Railway Express Company. He states that the Express Company had torn the rug in shipment and that it was badly damaged.

I declined, at least until Mr. Chamberlen, Manager of the Railway Express Company, a friend and also a good customer of mine, telephoned and asked me if I would inspect the rug for them.

It took very little time to recognize that the tears and breaks which Mr. E. was blaming on the Express Company were due to the rug being a saltwater damaged rug. Taking the rug in hand near the breaks and tears, I could, with very little effort, make similar tears and breaks in other places. Five husky men on each end of any rug could not do that to an oriental rug that was not saltwater damaged (or dry rot damaged).

For sixty years every importing house has carried insurance against this risk. I would not fail to have every one of the fifty shipments we have arriving from abroad each year so covered. (The risk is small today compared to forty years ago; better packing and better ships.)

The auction house which offered this damaged Kirman knew full well that this rug was damaged. The insurance company, you can be sure, had paid the importing company, and the insurance company had turned it over to a certain place for sale.

Of course, a few small jobbers in New York do not hesitate to buy these. In many cases they cut the rug and hope to cut out the damaged area, and still have a rug.

But the auction house had sold this rug to Mr. E. for $2000.00. At that time we were able to furnish Mr. E. an excellent and perfect Kirman in the size for $1250.00, much less than he paid at auction for the damaged Kirman.

I do not mean to say that all rugs offered at Atlantic City at auction are damaged rugs. But I could write a fancy book about some deals from there over the years, and we have the living proof of prominent people to whom it happened. Mr. E's lawyer, I believe, eventually got his $2000.00 back.

AUCTION OF ESTATES

Buying an oriental rug at auction of a wealthy estate is no insurance that your rug will be a valuable or desirable rug. Of course, you go, but do you know what you are doing? I would much prefer to see you buy the rug at a private sale of the estate.

We have seen dozens of the richest estates where the majority of the oriental rugs, for which huge prices had been paid, were both chemically washed and painted. Again I remind you that from 1905 to 1955 more than half of all orientals were both chemically washed and painted (see my chapter on this in my large book).

This doesn't mean that these rugs do not have some good value as floor covering. But they never become more valuable, and are always less valuable each year. They never interest the student of oriental rugs.

Only from a collector's estate, or the estate of a real student of antique rugs, will you find an entire collection of good rugs.

But, regardless of where you go to buy, you will do well to *use the check points on my list.*

I would hate to tell you of the many times that yours truly, the so-called expert, has made many costly mistakes in looking at rugs in the homes, and setting a price we would pay, then to find that once on our floors in our store, I had missed many defects. If I had been more careful and seen all the defects, I would have offered, say, $300.00 instead of $500.00. It is difficult to inspect a large rug in the home with furniture on it.

In one case, where the couple had both been in a nursing home for a year, I offered $325.00 for an 8 × 11 ft. rug. When one of my men pulled it from under the sofa and was about to roll it to bring in, he saw that the back was all moth-eaten on that side. It was not worth even $50.00 to us.

Our check list will help you, but it will not keep you from making some mistakes.

If you must go to the auction, be sure and go at the time they are open for inspection, and under no circumstances put in a bid on a rug that you have not had the opportunity to examine carefully.

Of course, a bid of $50.00 to $100.00, provided you have fun and are willing to charge much of it to entertainment, is fine. Unless you need to stretch every dollar, this will not hurt you.

KNOWLEDGEABLE WOMAN FROM INDIANA

Before closing our discussion on auctions, I want to offer a letter from a customer of mine in Hammond, Indiana. This lady has made quite a study of oriental rugs and has written a very fine article on oriental rugs that was published in a magazine.

It is amazing that many people do not have her good judgment. I wish I could print her fine article. The following is a letter which she wrote me and I have permission to print it and use her name. But, I have decided not to use her name.

"Dear Mr. Jacobsen:
I thought you might be interested in this article which appeared in our local newspaper last week. They are the same people that were here once before several months ago. The only difference was that they advertised their address as Indianapolis, Indiana, but we took a drive around back and noticed that the license plates were still Washington, D. C. I can't understand why they would return to this area after such a poor turn-out

last time they were here. We went to the preview. The big names, Nain, Kashan, Kirman, etc., were just leaders. They had one Nain rug, good quality, and one Kashan, of the most inferior quality I ever saw. You would not believe that our rug and this one were even of the same family. The color and texture were poor and there was no intricacy at all. The weave looked like a poor Hamadan in the Kashan design. I was not aware that they ever made Kashans so poorly, unless this was another type rug woven in the Kashan design, and they tried to sell it under the Kashan name. Almost the entire bulk of rugs were Hamadans of the poorest quality you could imagine. Needless to say, we did not return for the auction.

It is a shame that people like this are free to travel the country ruining the name of oriental rugs. I can see how people could be taken in with these rugs, buy them and later become very discouraged. People still seem to be under the impression they are going to find a rare buy. I learned a long time ago, you pay for quality, and there is no way around it.

Thank you again.

Sincerely,
S. T."

RESUME

To recapitulate our thoughts and advice on auctions:

ONE—Avoid the itinerant auctioneers. The biggest gamble of all.

TWO—If your city has a permanent auction house and also an oriental rug store, or an oriental rug department in a large store, my advice is to go there instead of the auction house. Your auction house has overhead expenses the same as the rug dealer. It stands to reason that the rug dealer buys more rugs, knows more about rugs, because he specializes in them, than the auctioneer, and you should make a better buy from him than from the auctioneer.

You have no chance of getting a rare buy at an auction because the rug is not going to be knocked down until it reaches a profitable price. Barest chance is when these permanent auction houses get the rugs from an estate. Make sure you inspect them carefully before the auction. Our check list will help you.

The best-known auction house in New York, and perhaps in the world, does get great works of art and some great rugs from time to time. If you are one of the rich millionaires and not one of the poor millionaires, you will have your own expert at such a sale to advise you.

The one auction you might want to attend is that of an estate. But here this can be a gamble unless you know that the rugs are actually a part of the estate. So often rugs, which are not part of the estate, are brought in to swell the sale.

I have great respect for a well-known auctioneer in Garrison, New York, who conducts auctions of some very large estates. Even though his fee is 20%, he provides everything necessary for his auction—advertising, mailing, etc. He gives some very good advice to those attending auctions, and I quote:

"If you are an amateur, study the subject you are interested in. Read up on it . . . check values by going to dealers. . . .

"BE SURE IT'S A LEGITIMATE AUCTION BY CHECKING BANKS OR ESTATE SOURCES. THERE ARE A LOT OF FAKES, WHERE A HOUSE IS RENTED FOR AN AUCTION AND FILLED WITH JUNK.

Go to the exhibit which precedes the auction with someone experienced, if possible, for appraisal. Don't listen to the person next to you at the auction. . . ." End of quote.

The above is good advice. If you are going to an estate auction, investigate and make sure the rugs are, in fact, part of the household goods actually used in that home.

Chapter Five

USED RUG SALES

I certainly recommend your buying a good used rug or even an imperfect rug at a price, but I do not recommend your buying these at one of the big "USED RUG SALES" at one of the large stores that continually run them as their principal way of selling oriental rugs.

You will generally do better at an oriental rug dealer who conducts a business without resorting to the exaggerated ads run in most used rug sales.

DIFFERENCE BETWEEN ANTIQUE, SEMI-ANTIQUE AND USED RUGS

The term "used rugs" needs some clarification. This is especially true when you go to a used rug sale as advertised by most of the big stores. Looking down the list you will see scores of the rugs listed as "excellent," and names that were never made 40 or 50 years ago—definitely new rugs—and too many times the poorer quality of that name.

This is one of the unethical practices that we object to in these used rug sales. They do not have enough used rugs, so they pad them with new rugs which, to my mind, is clearly a deception and an unethical practice.

While it is true that all antique and semi-antique rugs are in a sense and in reality used rugs, few dealers include the choice ones and those in good condition as used rugs. They were either used in Persia but mostly in America, and there would be no such classification as antique if we put them all as used.

The above is our classification. An ordinary antique, slightly worn or worn, would be classified as used. All chemically washed and painted rugs are always classified as used, even if used only a year. All Chinese

45

rugs, with the exception of a very few antiques, are definitely classified as used. Any of the rugs from India that have been used are definitely classified as used rugs.

So, mainly, a used rug, unless it is rare, is one that is somewhat worn and not in good condition.

SOURCES OF USED RUGS

The regular store dealer will acquire his used rugs either in trade or by purchase from his customers in his community. He will have renovated them himself at much less cost than those to be bought from the jobbers of used rugs in the New York wholesale district. Most of the rugs offered on "Used Rug Sales" by the stores specializing in this (and there are some great stores in New York that resort to these "Used Rug Sales") come from the small jobbers in the New York wholesale market. Their prices are prohibitive. They have been spoiled by European buyers who purchase any rare rug that comes along. There is not one chance in a hundred that a rare antique will be found in one of these used rug sales.

A few years ago, I bought hundreds of good used rugs from these small jobbers in New York, but since the advent of European buyers and the "Used Rug Sales" by these large stores, it is a waste of time to even visit with them. As a rule, they actually want more from me at wholesale than we are willing to sell them for at retail to our customers. Since most used rug sales in the large stores in the cities over the country are put on by some operator in New York, and if not, at least the rugs are brought in from the New York market, there is little chance of your finding a choice used rug at a good price, or any poor used rug at a bargain price.

And I repeat that your local dealer or large store who actually gets his used rugs in trade or by purchase locally, will offer you a better buy.

We, ourselves, acquire somewhere between 1,000 to 2,000 used rugs in trade each year or by purchase from old customers. We do a better job of renovating these, refinishing sides and edges, making small repairs in the field, at less than half of what New York repairmen would charge us. And we do a better job. AND MAKE SURE WE TELL YOU THE EXACT CONDITION OF THE RUG.

And, we believe, most retail dealers over the country will do better renovating than you will find on any "USED RUG SALE."

I believe there has been a letup in the used rug sales by many

Plate 15. ANTIQUE BERGAMO from Turkey, about 3 × 4 ft. An ancient Bergamo. Picture would indicate it older than the same type rug (design, size) in a number of museums. The change of color is not too objectionable, but this rug, from a collector's point of view, is one of the least desirable of this type that we have seen, and is worth, in its condition, probably $40.00. The beginner might well pay several times this on a used rug sale for the type.

stores. The three main reasons for this letup in the "Used Rug Sale" fever, or gimmick, all over the country is shortage of used rugs at reasonable prices; the fact they are not as successful as they were a few years ago; and the fact they have had so many complaints and returns, that many stores have discontinued such sales.

USED RUG SALES ADS—THE GIMMICK
FOR VOLUME

But one large store in New York continues with every ad (every ad of theirs I have seen in the *New York Times* over the past several years —perhaps they have run others) with used rug sale headlines. And another huge store continues with used rugs ads a number of times each year.

New York stores can get away with such sales better than dealers in

47

smaller towns. Returning the rug or getting an adjustment often becomes a chore, requiring more than one trip to the office or management in most cases, so that oftentimes the customer gives up. The fact that these sales have continued for some ten years would indicate that they have an appeal to many and that they are a financial success.

I will cite a few typical cases of such transactions, but only of those on which we have documented proof, letters, and receipts.

One of these large stores (I think without exception) has had one combination importer and rug dealer furnish all the rugs for these sales over the years. This man tags each rug with name and price before they are sent to the store for the sale. The store gets 33-1/3%, or 1/3 of the selling price. For example, on a $150.00 rug, the store gets $50.00 and the dealer gets the $100.00, and he has to make his own profit out of the $100.00. Wouldn't you believe that every used rug or new rug on that sale has to be sold at double the cost for him to make a profit?

The other large store which runs many used rug sales, and like most every one of these sales includes many new rugs, goes to the used rug dealers and many importers, and selects rugs to be sent to the store for the used rug sales. The rule is that each dealer must price and mark a certain percentage price on each rug (the tag) before it is sent to the store.

When I read, in the ad, how these rugs have been selected by their expert buyer of many years I am amazed, after having watched groups of rugs being sent out by the different dealers to this store for the sale.

Just how much these statements mean, you can make your own estimates after I give you, later on, a few cases of disenchanted buyers who asked this store to take the rugs back or to at least exchange them.

EXORBITANT PRICES ON USED RUGS
IN THE WHOLESALE MARKET

Every month or two, with the great need on our part for good used rugs, I go to an old friend of mine in New York City who used to deal almost entirely in new rugs from Iran, and he did very well.

For the past several years he has gone into the used rug business, accumulating them for sales to send on consignment to New York stores, and to sell the best ones to Europe. Time after time, I have taken an hour or two with one of my top assistants and we have looked at a few hundred of his large stock of used rugs. A few times we have bought as many as three rugs from him, but the hundreds of others would be either washed and painted, too worn, and practically every one of them would be quite thin. Many had already been doctored up by painting in the worn areas. But, among the great number, possibly there would be ten to twenty rugs, even though thin, we would have liked to buy. The prices were impossibly high—actually, much higher than we would let you pay us.

And this, and other such places with the same general situation, are the sources of rugs for the used rug sales.

So, what I am saying is that most of the used rugs offered will be of some value, and about half of them are good looking. But the prices of these are so out of line for our standards, and, I believe, the standards of most of the smaller dealers over the country.

Remember, you can buy your used rugs at a better price from the dealer who gets his used rugs by taking them in trade or buying them from his customers.

Also, remember that many of the rugs offered on used rug sales are actually new rugs. I know that many of them have some of the bad faults that we have outlined in our check list of new rugs. Perhaps many good rugs are included. But that does not mean that one of these new rugs on a used rug sale, even with defects, is not a good buy if the price is right, and you are satisfied with the colors, defects and all.

The fact that a new rug is badly clipped or that it is very irregular in shape, or that there are radical changes of colors, or has some of the other faults listed in our check list, does not mean that at a price it is not a good buy, provided the customer likes it. Such a rug will last perhaps a lifetime and be less expensive per year by far than most machine made rugs or broadloom. Unfortunately, the prices are generally higher than you can buy a better rug of the same type for in most reliable oriental rug stores.

People go to used rug sales looking for bargains or soft colors. And they go to find certain sizes they need which their dealer does not have. If it is the inexpensive rug or bargain you are seeking, then buy one of these new rugs with faults if the price is right. As a rule it will be a better buy than the badly worn used rug, or the used washed and painted rug, or the worn-out rug that has been doctored up with paint to hide the worn spots. No fault is quite as bad as the rug with the back moth-eaten and which has been hidden by touching with dye. There is one way to make this usable for a good many years, and that is by using Lastex on the back of the moth-eaten places, but this destroys most of the resale value of the rug.

SAFER TO BUY FROM A REGULAR RUG DEALER

The regular dealer will usually sell you a better rug at the same price paid at a used rug sale.

What I am trying to say is that these used rug sales greatly exaggerate the merits of the rugs offered. I am a firm believer that each of these used rugs and each new rug with faults will sell more readily and make more friends, if the dealer will point out the defects and faults, and say that is why the rug has a low price.

Unfortunately, the low price does not exist as a rule for the rug offered on these used rug sales.

FEWER EUROPEAN BUYERS

The demand by European buyers for our used rugs has diminished tremendously since 1966. For several years you daily ran into a dozen retail dealers, even wholesale dealers, from Europe combing the New York market for old rare rugs.

These European dealers are pretty well loaded with rugs for which they paid dearly to the American dealers; in most every case far more than most of the American dealers could sell these at retail.

But the exportation did not stop until these European dealers had carted off a large percentage of the rarest rugs which retail dealers all over the country and jobbers in the New York market had accumulated over the years. My guess is that it will take a good many years for American dealers to replenish from estates the rare rugs they sold to Europe, if it is at all possible to replenish them.

The European buyers may be finding the selling of these rugs, at prices they ask for them, not so easy. I have not inspected the shops in Germany and other countries on the Continent in the past few years, but I have been in a number of London stores and find great numbers of old rugs at unbelievably high prices. I am not going to mention names of the few rugs that I remember at $1500.00 to $2500.00 for the 4×6 ft. size in a type that in America would be considered very high, even with today's scarcity, at $1000.00. In the condition I saw one Feraghan displayed in a window at $1800 (worn right down), we, here in the States, would think in terms of about $300.00.

At the big bonded government warehouse in London, a wholesale market for European buyers, I saw hundreds of old rugs that had come from America. Time after time, after going through their importations from Iran, etc., I would see a rug or several rugs (rolled) and ask the dealer what they were and if they were in good condition. The dealer would say, "That is not for you; they came from America." The implication was that they had overpaid for the rug.

I actually believe that many of these dealers are beginning to realize that they made mistakes in paying such high prices, and that it is going to take several years to work off their overpriced American-bought antiques.

Now, again I would like to repeat that I am certainly not against buying a used rug, not even a badly worn one, if it looks presentable and is priced right. Time after time I say that a used rug in good condition is to be preferred as a rule to a new rug of the same type.

"Then why are you hollering your head off against these used rugs sales?" someone may well ask.

Again, my chief objection is to the overstatement and exaggerations as to the merits of the rugs and the off-color practice of including hundreds of new rugs and listing them as used with the condition listed as E (excellent). Perhaps I do not want to be put in the same class in my line of business.

RANK EXAGGERATIONS

Overstatements are so apparent to every dealer and importer alike. Take, for example, such advertisements as: "Fabulous rugs from great estates—rare museum pieces"; "Like museum pieces, used oriental rugs are rare and valuable"; and "Our store has a veritable museum of treasured oriental rugs."

Of course, these statements are rank exaggerations. I wish you might have heard the remarks and the disgust on the part of dozens of real collectors or people who had some knowledge of rare rugs. I have always thought of a rug graded as a collector's item to be "a superior rug of the type, or the particular weave; the best or among the very best of each type."

But certain named rugs are seldom considered as collectors' items. Listing of names like Sparta, Lillihan, Beloochistans, Ardebils, and many others as collectors' items tells the story to any collector or rug man.

Today came yesterday's ad in the *New York Times*, and I will not be cruel enough to reprint the awful exaggerations and claims. Makes one a little ashamed to tell anyone he is an oriental rug dealer. To reprint the line would name the store as they have used these great claims for years in almost the identical statements each time.

51

But I must call your attention to the column listing "Collector's Items," in the Used Rug Sales. Some 22 of the rugs listed are small "Belouj," barely larger than 3 × 5 ft. at $115.00 each. In the first place, Belouj (Beloochistan, Baluchistan) would be one of the least sought-after types as a collector's item. A collector would want a Beloochistan only if it was super-quality, old with lovely natural sheen; just being an old Beloochistan isn't enough for a collector. These offered are hardly old enough to be called semi-antiques.

Is there a collector or dealer so naive that he would dare say that in one offering there would be 22 antiques in this quality? At best they were average semi-antique rugs. The quality that we would think of as being collector's quality would never appear in numbers, but will appear one or two at a time, and over a period of a year, perhaps a total of six rare top grade ones would show up.

Everyone in the trade knows full well that this was a group of Beloochistans (Belouj, if he wants to spell it that way, is no harm) that had been bought as a group, and were new or at best, semi-old.

Their only justification could be that a collection to this store means a number of different types of rugs. But a collector's rug of any item must be one in many hundreds, and very choice.

And we count 17 listings of Ardebil rugs from Northern Iran in this same collector's column. While they copy the old Caucasian designs, every dealer knows that these are Persians and that it is only since World War II that these have been woven in this type, copying the Caucasian designs.

Of course, they bought them from the New York or Teheran market, all new with the bare exception of two or three having a few years' usage. These are very nice rugs, and some are better than others, but not collector's items.

SELDOM A REAL COLLECTOR'S ITEM

I have inspected thousands of these and bought a few hundred over the years, but I do not think we could maintain our reputation if we classed these as collector's items.

Also, in this same Collector's Column, they listed Aroon (a few of these). Every importer and dealer knows that this is the lower grade of Kashan. They are all right at a price, and good looking, even if one-fourth as fine as the best Kashan, but who would ever class one of these as a collector's item?

These three items covered about half of those listed as collector's items. And looking at the prices of each of these, it is safe to say that regarding just about every item listed in this column, you could buy the same type, equally as good, from the regular stock of any store or dealer at the price or less.

Every collector knows the thirty to forty principal names that interest a collector. A real collector would hardly have a rug by the names so listed by this store.

And from my own observation and more especially from letters from dozens of people, not one of them found what they considered a collector's item among the rugs advertised. In fact, I doubt if you could induce one of the real experts ever again to visit such a sale. Their remarks are more caustic than mine.

Appreciating how difficult it is to find new rugs in soft colors, except the high-priced Kirmans (lightly bleached) and the rugs from India, I would not write any criticism of these used rug sales provided these stores would say that any rug bought, after being in your home for two days, can be returned for credit, or at least for exchange. It is true that many buyers of these rugs do manage to return some of them even though these ads often say "All sales final—no C.O.D.s and no returns."

These used rug sales, instead of being a thorn in my side (they give us no competition as none are held in central New York) are a boon to our business. Hundreds and hundreds of people from the Metropolitan Area of New York, from New Jersey and Connecticut, who would normally shop in the New York City area, come to Syracuse to buy their oriental rugs often because they have lost confidence in some of the stores elsewhere.

RECOMMENDED ETHICS

I repeat over and over that the used rug is fine and the used rug sale would be all right if three factors were eliminated and one was added. These are the elimination of (1) the exaggerated claims for the rugs; (2) the overpricing of these rugs; (3) the inclusion of so many new rugs, marking them as condition E (excellent), leading the reader to believe that they are used rugs.

And most important, there should be an agreement or understanding that any rug selected could be returned after it was received in the home if objectionable features were discovered.

But this is not to condemn the majority of used rugs offered, provided there is an honest indication of their condition and that prices are realistic.

As much as I dislike any chemically washed and painted rug (even though most good stores sold them and liked the process when it was in use generally), even a used rug so treated which is not completely worn out could be good floor covering to many people, and I would not blame the store for selling them at a price. But never could they sell them to people who have lived with antiques, semi-antiques, or natural colored new orientals.

I say that a used rug sale containing nothing but used rugs, or an ad with part of the ad listing a limited number of used rugs would be fine.

And I remind you that hardly one of these New York stores will take a used rug in trade on another oriental rug you purchase from them. The method is to bring these in on consignment for the period of the sale, and those not sold are then returned to the owners.

A FEW TYPICAL PURCHASES

As I write, so many cases and sad experiences by people who have bought at these sales come to mind. No doubt, for every one who has had a bad experience many others were happy or satisfied; otherwise, these sales could not have continued in such vogue during the past ten years.

It would take a wicked pen to detail the many cases that have been brought to our attention. But I will give you two or three examples of actual experiences of which we have records or letters that these cusomers have written.

The first comes from the great store that advertises so strongly that their expert of many years has established and appraised the value of the used rugs offered.

As I punch this out in my Florida home (Naples) in this delightful town, three blocks away in a lovely mansion on the beach lives a prominent man who came from the Metropolitan Area of New York. He is now a City Councilman and Vice Mayor, and, incidentally, a nice man who would not complain about a small thing.

I recall that a few years ago, en route to Syracuse to see his mother, he stopped off in New York and went to the used rug sale of this store. He bought a used 9×12 ft. Mahal for $295.00. He had also bought a new Pakistan Bokhara, barely larger than $4\frac{1}{2} \times 6\frac{1}{2}$ ft., for $275.00. Here the price is important, because from anyone's regular stock he could have bought the same rug for $150.00 to $195.00. And we actually sold him one we thought much prettier and more desirable for $150.00, or half the price he paid in the sale for the same type new Bokhara.

This was late summer and his home was being completed. By the time we arrived in Naples he had moved in his new home and had just put down the used 9×12 ft. rug on the floor. He and his wife were disappointed with this rug and had no idea of leaving it on their floor, even if they had to lose the full price. They telephoned me and asked if I would come over, and I drove over the three short blocks.

I, too, was horrified at what I saw. The old Mahal was badly worn out, with very little but the base or warp and weft remaining, and hardly any nap anywhere, especially in the field. The small dealer who had given it to the store on consignment had dabbed dye all over the field. To anyone's eye it would have been a worn-out piece of junk before being dyed. The dealer who furnished the rug to the store for the sale did not even take time to do a good job of touching. How my friends could have failed to see these things in the store is hard to understand. But once in their home the painting showed up badly, and it is hard to imagine anyone who would have lived with this atrocity, even had the price been $50.00 for the 9×12 ft. rug.

So this is the kind of value and expert appraisal this store advertises their buyer of many years makes.

And to add a final note, the identical rug had been sent to me for a trade-in from a customer in Pennsylvania and we allowed $15.00 for the rug and would not have taken it at any price except for the sizable purchase the customer was making from us.

I believe we sold it to the little dealer in New York for $20.00 who, in turn, touched it (painted in the design) and no doubt gave it to the store on consignment for $200.00, and placed a price tag on it of $295.00 so the store would get 33%, or about $100.00 of the selling price.

Now, I am sure this is an exaggerated case, and most of the complaints are minor compared to this one.

My friend who had bought the rug wrote to the president of the big store and told him he had bought it as a used rug on sale and had not been able to try it on his floor until his house was ready. But he could not use it, and told him what they had discovered. This gentleman had been a good customer of this store for years, and, I am happy to report that he got his check for $295.00 back in full.

A TRULY TRAGIC AND DISGRACEFUL CASE

I want to give you one other very bad case where this same store which advertises that their rugs are so carefully appraised and valued by their expert of many years, sold three rugs to a doctor. We have a thirty page file on this with the actual letters or photostatic copies from the doctor and from the store.

It concerns a leading doctor at one of the world's most famous clinics in the Midwest; we will call him Dr. X.

Dr. X was a customer of ours for many years, but one year, recently when I was in Florida, he wrote to my store three times but got no answer. I could never explain why my truly great expert could have failed to contact and offer him rugs. (This man of mine is deceased, so I will say no more except that his failure was inexcusable.) If he had a backlog of letters, at least he could have phoned our doctor customer.

Dr. X, being in New York at a medical meeting, and seeing the full page ad in the *New York Times*, "Used Rug Sale," by this large store, went there and bought three oriental carpets, two approximately 9 × 12 ft., and one barely larger, paying some $1550.00 cash for the three rugs.

These were duly shipped to his home where he did not unbale them for over a month, waiting until his new home was completed.

Returning to Syracuse from Florida, I discovered my man's failure to answer Dr. X's request for rugs, and I immediately telephoned him my apology. He stated the rugs were not unrolled, and that he knew it was so unlike me not to answer his letters. He assured me he would want other rugs and would contact me personally.

A few weeks later he telephoned me and wrote me, giving me the sad news to the effect that when the three orientals, bought at the used rug sale at this large store in New York City were laid on the floor, his wife and daughter were actually horrified. I recall his saying that in all his 25 years of married life this was the first bad feeling his wife had ever registered against him. "How could he pay $1550.00 for three such horrible looking rugs?" They would not let them stay on the floors next to the rugs he already owned, even overnight.

He stated that I had to help him out and that he would be willing to take a real loss if I could take them in on suitable rugs.

I told him I did not think the situation could be quite as bad as he pictured it. One rug was a Sarouk, and it immediately occurred to me it probably was a bright new Sarouk that we could sell as we do other new Sarouks. I knew Mrs. X wanted only soft colors, i.e., semi-antiques or antiques.

So the three rugs arrived—and there is no way to cover this subject with the full picture without being long-winded.

First, there was a Sparta, or Anatolian rug in the Persian design, with the old machine-made appearance which, you will note by reading my large book in the chapter on Turkish rugs, I have never liked, and neither have 99 out of 100 of my customers. This was a second quality, about Nazar quality, at $1.25 per square foot wholesale (back many years ago when they were being made).

Dr. X had paid $350.00 for this rug. This was the best of the lot and worth what one was willing to pay for it—in my book the extreme maximum of $195.00. My top assistant had one almost identical in design, condition, and quality, which he had sold that day for $69.00. But this rug was a typical value in one of these used rug sales. I could not help the dear doctor on this. And this was the least serious complaint regarding the three rugs.

The next rug, about $8\frac{1}{2} \times 12$ ft. Meshed from Iran, illustrates one of the real dangers and deceptions we warn about in our check list. It was an old Meshed rug (call it Ispahan Meshed if you wish). First, the outside borders had been removed, evidently by reason of being moth-eaten, or at least for some cogent reason the edge was the wide main border. This in itself, while reducing the value, would not destroy some good value of the rug if it did not have too many other serious faults.

But it demonstrated the unforgivable and rottenest trick that can be played on you with a used rug, namely, being worn flat down to the warp. The background had been painted in and there was nothing in considerable areas of the rug but painted-in warp and weft.

Of course, Dr. X was not told this, and perhaps only the small jobber who had done the painting and faking knew it, but be sure he knew it when he priced it for $350.00 and sent it over on consignment for the sale. The store's buyer was very poor in his appraisal, and failure in not recognizing this.

Even a piece of junk like this has some value for one who wants to buy the semblance of an oriental rug for a few dollars, and oftentimes these will go along quite a few years and will be less expensive over that period than the wall to wall affair.

Here is where the real danger is, too often, on these used rug sales: a rug that should have sold for $50.00 to $95.00 was sold to the trusting and unsuspecting doctor for $350.00.

But the real gyp, and off-colored part of the transaction, was the third rug: a saltwater damaged, chemically washed and painted Sarouk for which the good doctor paid $950.00. He could have bought a perfect, new Sarouk in the size for less at any good store. Knowing that the New York market would buy, and does not object to, the chemical washing and painting process, and since we boast that we have never sold such rugs in all our forty-five years, I shipped the rug to a close friend in the trade in New York who is perhaps as well-known and as highly regarded as any man in the New York wholesale market. As you know, saltwater damage results in weak and rotten spots.

Upon receipt, he immediately phoned me, and in just about these words, said, "Colonel, that Sarouk of your doctor friend is a saltwater-damaged rug, and has some 25 repaired or reinforced places, if you look on the back of the rug."

I did not know, and had not examined it on the underside as I should have. I simply assumed that it was a new washed and painted rug.

And, he continued, "This rug came from our good friends, Importers B, and you know them well enough to know that they did not give it to Store A as a new perfect rug, or as a used rug, but as a damaged rug."

I cannot use the name because the same friend furnishes this store many used rugs for their sales, which was the reason I shipped it to him.

So here the good doctor had paid a high price for a new Sarouk (at least $150.00 more than most stores would sell it for at a 40% gross), and he had not only gotten one chemically washed and painted, but one that had been saltwater damaged en route from Iran, and for which the importing house had no doubt collected their insurance.

The question is, did the expert, whom Store A advertises so carefully selects the rugs they offer, slip up in his inspection, or did he try to make a killing on a damaged rug he got on consignment for little money?

I gave the facts to the good doctor. He then wrote a personal letter to the *President* of the great Store A, explaining what he had learned about the rugs, and stating that he intended buying old rugs, but he had no idea they were so bad and worn until he got them in his home and his wife refused to use them. What could he do? Could he trade?

To make a long story short, he took a loss of $300.00 on this purchase and was glad to lose only $300.00.

Pretty sad story, isn't it? And here is what the executive assistant to the President of Store A wrote our doctor. He said they approved of the chemical washing and painting process. That was enough to run away most people who had studied rugs a few hours. He completely ignored the real indictment of this deal, the fact that this rug was saltwater-damaged, and had many rotten spots reinforced which were plainly visible on the underside of the rug.

Sorry to impose all this on my good readers, but the intimate details are necessary if you are to be fully informed. As I said in the beginning, it would take a painful pen to list and detail the many unfortunate purchases that have been made at these used rug sales.

I am sure that the majority of rugs sold at these sales are not as bad as the above, and that there are many new rugs included in these sales. All I am trying to point out is that it is, in my humble opinion, more of a gamble to buy any rug on one of these "Used Rug Sales" than in going to another store and buying a good used rug that has been taken in trade, or buying the same type new rug that is included in the sale in a store that doesn't advertise "Used Rug Sale!"

It is hard to understand why or how a large department store, for instance, in a city the size of Rochester, will let an outside dealer come in and put on a used rug sale for a limited time. This store, to the best of my knowledge, has never in 45 years had a regular oriental rug department. Is it because another department store there does have an oriental rug department? Is it because it brings them a good volume of sales?

Since they have held these "Used Rug Sales" for the past few years, they must make sizable sales, but I don't believe that the great image of that old store is being helped. And I wonder if the few thousand dollars volume is worth the damage they do to their store. I have heard so many disparaging remarks about this store's oriental rugs sales. I know many stores over the country have stopped these mainly because of the returns for credit when the faults are discovered in the rugs after they are in the purchasers' homes.

Plate 16. ANTIQUE PRAYER LAVER KIRMAN from Iran, using the unusual tree-of-life design covering the field. Many collectors like to refer to these as "bird" rugs, but we prefer the term "Laver," referring to the rarest of Kirmans. Such rugs have not been imported during the past fifty years and will not be found in a used rug sale. Even a thin one is valuable. Definitely a collector's item. Sice 6.9 × 4.3 feet. *(Courtesy of Mr. L. C. Decbar, New Orleans)*

Plate 17. ANTIQUE SHIRVAN from Caucasia, with the effulgent star design over the field and the crab design in the main border. In perfect condition. The slight change of color shown in this rug at one end in no way hurts its value as a rare collector's item. Field very much like that in Plate 162 in our earlier book, the original of which is in the Metropolitan Museum. Size 5.1 × 3.8 feet. *(Courtesy of Mr. L. C. Deckbar, New Orleans)*

Chapter Six

DETAILED DISCUSSION OF CHECK POINTS IN BUYING A NEW ORIENTAL RUG

It is assumed you will heed our TWO MOST IMPORTANT ADMONITIONS: One—NEVER BUY AN ORIENTAL RUG at auction sales (itinerant auctions); Two—BE OVER CAUTIOUS in buying a rug "new" or "used" at a "USED RUG SALE."

Here is a check list that can help the beginner—the buyer of his first few rugs. We think it will help even the average rug dealer and those with a good deal of experience in buying oriental rugs. It will even help us if we make sure to check out each of these points listed below.

Again, did someone ask why should one have to check for faults in a new oriental rug?

We NEED to impress you AGAIN and AGAIN that a good percentage of the new oriental rugs imported from Iran (Persia) have bad objectionable faults. While handmade rugs are not supposed to be perfect, like machine made rugs, and small things should not be objectionable, it is a definite fact that too many rugs from Iran are coming in with very bad faults.

Practically every new rug requires some small attention after it is received. These are not objectionable faults but they are minor deficiencies that should be corrected by the retail dealer when you buy a rug. I refer particularly to poor overcasting of the sides, to wrinkling along the edges, and edges being curled under on finely woven rugs. These minor things are easily corrected, but not one in five new rugs sold have these corrections made.

The serious faults seldom apply to many types. They especially apply to the rugs from the Hamadan District, and more so to some of the rugs from this district than others. The Kapoutarhang, a medium quality rug, has deteriorated to the point where we reject three out of four of these. The Kasvins, one of our favorite rugs, are being rejected in num-

Figure 3. Misshapen rugs. The left rug can be made straight by sizing. The middle rug can be improved some by sizing, but is definitely too crooked to bring the full price. The rug on the right with one corner tent-shaped is often objectionable. This sketch shows slight irregularity which can be pulled straight, but an exaggerated case of this is definitely objectionable.

bers because of bad clipping. By careful inspection we still can find good ones, though not nearly enough of these.

While there has been a great deterioration in the goods from the Hamadan District, a district that supplies over one-third of the rugs coming to America from Iran, there has been a great improvement in many types coming from other sections of Iran.

Not in the history of weaving, during the past 200 years, have there been many rugs woven to equal the wonderful Nains that we are getting in limited numbers today.

The contract-quality Kirman, so-called 80/40 quality, is far better than most Kirmans woven 30 years before World War II. They come with few faults.

The Sarouks, after deteriorating in quality in order to hold the price line, have improved in a number of ways. We can thank the Germans for this. We criticized them for running prices up and taking the Sarouk market away from Americans, but this proved to be a blessing in disguise from my point of view, because they improved the designs and the

Figure 4.   Misshapen rugs. Left rug with a bad nose is objectionable. Sizing will cure some of it. Rug at right is entirely too crooked and the value greatly reduced thereby.

quality. See our discussion in Chapter Eight, "Changes During Past Eight Years," or since the publication of my large book, *Oriental Rugs— A Complete Guide* in 1962.

The Gorevans and Herez reached a very low level some ten years ago, but again the Germans, who favor these rugs, have been mainly responsible for the elimination of the junky type that was to be found in great numbers at almost every importing house. You do not see one of these today, only very good to excellent quality. Of course, some of these, and some of most types, can have serious faults, but it is mainly the new rugs from the Hamadan District that you will have to check carefully.

OUR DETAILED DISCUSSION WILL ALERT YOU TO MANY DEFICIENCIES, BUT THEY SHOULD NOT UNDULY ALARM YOU—ONLY HELP YOU.

THERE ARE PLENTY OF WONDERFUL ORIENTAL RUGS TO BE HAD, AND ANY GOOD DEALER WILL CORRECT ANY SMALL FAULT YOU FIND IN THE RUG AFTER IT IS IN YOUR HOME, OR, IF THE FAULT IS SERIOUS, HE WILL REPLACE THE RUG. A GOOD DEALER WILL SELDOM MISS A SERIOUS FAULT.

1. IS THE RUG VERY IRREGULAR IN SHAPE? TOO CROOKED?

This is a very important point to many people, but it is the least important of all the points we discuss.

One does not have to be an expert to detect the crookedness once the rug is in their home. No one can prescribe an exact rule as to when a rug is too crooked or too irregular in shape. Much depends on the individual person.

I am not going to try to tell you what you should do on this point, but I will tell you the general rules we follow, and what the vast majority of our customers over the last 46 years have liked and what they have disliked.

You cannot expect a handmade oriental rug to be perfectly straight, or as straight as a machine-made domestic rug. But it is a fact that many new oriental rugs are so irregular in shape to the extent that nine out of ten prospective buyers would object.

You must not reject a rug in the dozar size (dozar is a rug approximately $4\frac{1}{2} \times 6\frac{1}{2}$ feet) simply because it is one to three inches wider at one end than at the other. This will not even be noticeable on your floors. We will usually reject a new rug in this size that varies as much as six inches in width at one end from the other.

But it is a fact that many people will not object even to this six inches or more variance, and say frankly, "This makes the rug more oriental to me." Most of the people tell us this especially when they already own the rug and are interested in trading or selling the rug.

We buy what nine out of ten will not object to, and we admit that we are known in the trade as being too particular on this point.

Again, remember we are discussing new rugs from Iran, Pakistan and Afghanistan. The rugs from India are almost without exception perfectly straight.

You will seldom find a carpet size, 8×10 feet or larger, that has exactly the same width at each end of the rug. Certainly, one to three inches variance in a 9×12 rug should make no difference to anyone. And in many cases a six inch variance will not be objectionable in a 9×12 foot or larger size rug.

My inspectors (we require two experienced people), who spread each rug out flat on the floor to check for crookedness and other defects, will usually want to return a rug which is off as much as six inches. On a very large rug even the six inches difference may not be objectionable.

Marked irregularities along the edges, wavy sides and sizable noses (in shape) along sides or ends are usually objectionable to most people. We would eliminate these unless the rug was exquisite in beauty and quality, and unless we thought we could partially correct the faults.

One irregularity that usually causes rejection in a new rug, is where one corner is tent-shaped and the length on one side of the rug is longer than the length on the other side. Here again, this is a matter of personal taste.

RUNNERS REQUIRE MORE CAUTION. Selecting Persian runners requires great care as these are usually used in halls and on staircases where the irregularities will be more noticeable because of its close proximity to the walls.

We reject runners that cannot be sized nearly straight. An inch variance will not matter; perhaps two inches will not be very noticeable. And you will be surprised how perfectly straight many of these runners, that seem somewhat hopeless, can be corrected by sizing.

We size every Persian (Iranian) runner that we sell locally, and we size each one before shipping it out of town.

You may be wondering why all this talk about so many of the runners being crooked. I, too, wonder, and truly wonder where they finally wind up—at auctions? in used rug sales?

I must give you a few extreme cases that I experienced a few months ago at one of the largest, most reliable importing houses, run by my good friends for forty-five years.

I saw a large pile of narrow Karaja runners, approximately $2 \times 5\frac{1}{2}$ feet. I pulled down the pile, hastily selecting some thirty which I thought slightly better and more beautiful than the others. I then had two of the porters quickly spread them out, and at first glance I discarded half of them, selecting fifteen and rejecting exactly the same number. Without actually seeing these little runners, it was impossible to visualize how very crooked they were. No cutting out V areas or cutting and sewing, much less sizing, could ever make these right.

A month later in this same large importing house, I was seeking some 8-ft. Karaja runners. My good friend, the actual buyer in Iran, said to me, "Colonel, don't select from those in the pile. I have three fresh bales just arrived and I will open them and you can have first selection." From the first bale of 20 Karaja runners we could find only 2 or 3 that were not very crooked. The same thing was true of the second and third bales. We selected 8 runners from the 60 in these bales, even though we needed 15 or 20. They were too irregular in shape, not just slightly irregular.

I wonder how these were disposed of. At auctions or used rug sales? Who would be willing to have these lie on their floors? Of course, they could have been corrected to some extent. Who had made these? I suppose children on small flat looms.

How had my friend, who does most of the buying, been foolish enough to buy these? Had he bought them without laying them out and inspecting them? Certainly this must have been the answer. Or had an agent of theirs bought them for our friends and they had to make the best of it?

The public has no idea of what the importer or the retail dealer is up against. There is seldom room at any one of the importing houses in New York to properly inspect each rug he buys. In one of the larger showrooms, where their rugs take up most of the space, usually there is reserved one or two areas for showing carpet size rugs. But after two or three are spread out, one on top of the other, I defy the best expert to be able to tell if the rug is straight. Bad irregularities can be seen, but to make the proper inspection the rug must be spread out alone on the floor. This cannot be done in most wholesale places.

These importing houses in New York are not slick operators; they are most reliable, and I, or anyone, can return a rug for credit for any reason after we have had it on our floors.

Buying abroad requires much more care, because once bought, there is no way of returning it.

When you buy a rug from a reliable retail store you run no risk unless they have a sale stating, "no approvals, no returns, all sales final." That is a sale or store to avoid in buying your oriental rug.

2. CHANGES OF COLOR

My book, *Oriental Rugs—A Complete Guide,* covers this subject in detail, in Chapter Seventeen, pages 125–127, inclusive.

Here again, it is a matter of individual taste and personality. You will not find as many shadings and changes in the new rugs as are to be found in old rugs. But there are still many rugs made well out in the country where all the wool is not on hand when the weaving of the rug is begun.

Many slight changes add to the beauty of the rug, but this is more applicable to old rugs than new rugs.

In many new rugs you will note that at one end the colors are somewhat lighter than at the other and that this is a gradual change from one end to the other. This does not hurt the value of the rug unless it actually detracts from the beauty, which is seldom the case.

Some rugs that have a light chemical washing, after they get to New York, to tone down their colors, often develop these changes due to the dyes being different, and a bad change of color can appear that detracts greatly. As a rule, the rug is not salable unless it is then sent back to the renovating plant for painting and rewashing. These changes we call hair brushes and these, without exception, are objectionable. They have a sickish faded-out look as compared to the rest of the rug.

Changes of color and shades woven into the rug are entirely different from the hair brushes and, as stated, often add rather than detract from the beauty of the rug. See quote from Victoria and Albert Museum in London on this subject in Chapter Seven, Check Point No. 7.

3. DOES THE RUG LIE FLAT?

We repeat that you should insist on the rug you buy being flat. Do not let any one tell you that the bad wrinkles will walk out.

We size every Persian rug and also all Bokharas from Pakistan and Afghanistan. We do not have to size many of the rugs from India. The rug, if it lies flat, will be even better if it is sized with a little cold water glue. You can not know this has been done after it has dried, as there is no appearance of glue. It simply has the effect of giving any rug, and especially a loosely woven rug, a little firmness, or body, not a real stiffness.

Why would a new oriental rug not lie flat?

It may simply be due to being folded in the store, or it may be due to the fold in shipment from Iran to America. These rugs are folded several times and are tightly packed. It is true that these folds do come out of their own accord when opened to air, but they have to be folded again at the importer's and later in the retail store.

But some rugs come with a little extra fullness along the sides, which, if not made flat, will result in small humps. These will not only be a nuisance and unsightly, but will wear through much faster than the rest of the rug. When the fullness is so great that it cannot be sized out, or when sized and it returns, as a rule there is only one cure, and that is to cut little wedges (triangles) out where the humps are.

The sizing is good for any rug, and in making the rug flat, a 9 × 12 ft. rug that is, say, four inches wider at one end, can readily have this reduced by two inches.

Our method of sizing is to lay the rug out, face (nap) side against the floor, and simply kick the fullness out with one's heel (we do have stretchers, but seldom use them), and fasten the rug to the floor with small brads. Our people can do a 9 × 12 ft. rug in this manner in fifteen minutes at most. The back is then wet with a cold water glue solution from a sprinkling can, and spread out smooth over the rug with an ordinary broom. The rug is fully dry by morning, and it takes another fifteen to twenty minutes to remove these tiny brads with a pair of pliers.

The old-fashioned way is still employed by most of my friends in the New York market. They tack the rug down with hammer and regular tacks (stainless steel to prevent rusting) and follow the same process of wetting the back with cold water sizing glue.

I cannot understand why they continue this old-fashioned method. It takes a good hour or longer to size a 9 × 12 ft. rug. The tack holes are much larger than the almost invisible pin holes the brads make. Do not be alarmed at the tack holes; they do not harm the rug and will disappear as a rule. It is the great time that the tack method requires. I believe the real reason why the importing houses and most retailers use the tack method is that they size a rug only when it is quite irregular. Most people would not bother to size one out of ten that we size. They size the rug only if it is badly crooked, and the tacks being heavier and stronger permit them to stretch a very crooked rug more than with the brads. A rug twelve inches wider on one end, on a very large rug, can be sized nearly straight. You will not find an average rug, even with the great pressure applied in pulling this very crooked rug, being torn.

4. EDGES CURLED UNDER
ON MANY TIGHTLY WOVEN RUGS

This is a fault that you will find only in the very finely or very tightly woven rugs. This will not occur on the many rugs from the Hamadan District, except, occasionally, on a Kasvin. It is apt to occur on a Kirman, and this was a common occurrence on even the best of Kirmans until recently. In the past three years, this fault has seldom been present in one of the better contract Kirmans. Many Sarouks will have this fault—the edges being curled under. Examine Qums, Ispahans, Tabriz, Niris, Sarabends, Kashans, for this fault and only a small percentage of these will have it. But, you do not want to get the one.

It is a difficult thing to correct. Sizing often will do it, but in only about half the cases. It is often necessary to wet the edges and hammer them flat on the underside of the rug.

And a long, hard process is to sew this from the back, a method any good repairman knows, but it is time-consuming.

As a rule, when we get a rug with this curled-under edge condition, unless we have bought it abroad, or need it very badly, we return the rug to the importer.

Otherwise, the one sure cure is to cut off the one-fourth inch to one inch along the edge of the rug, and do a complete overcasting of the edges. Generally, there is a very narrow border which will not disturb the looks of the rug, and which you will not miss or know that it had ever been there.

But the cost is great—never less than $1.00 a foot, and on a very fine rug, perhaps as much as $2.00 a running foot.

Years ago we could buy a tape which enclosed small blocks of lead. We have not been able to get this material since World War II, but if we could, or could get something similar, we would sew it along the edges (underside) of very finely woven rugs. It would cure these curled under edges.

5. IS THE RUG BADLY CLIPPED?

Does the rug have a thick nap in one area, and thin nap in other areas? This is a point that applies mostly to new rugs from the Hamadan District, woven there in the past several years. It concerns principally the Kasvins (one of our favorite rugs), and the Kaputarhangs, and to a lesser extent a very few of the better Kapoutarhangs now selling under the name of Ramishan (a new name appearing for the first time about five years ago).

I have not noticed this on any of the Ingelas, the Tajabads, the Hosseinabads, or the Dargezines. A very few of the Bibikabads may have the fault—maybe one in a hundred. Nor have we seen it on Sarouks, Herez, Kirmans or other Iranian rugs.

But it has been a very serious fault that has, in the past few years, been present in at least half of the Kasvins, and in a larger percentage of the Kapoutarhangs.

I think the public is often more expert than we are, because the first time this came to our attention was from a few customers who called to say that there were bumps in the rug—that the nap in some places was higher than in others. It was not serious at first because, although by carefully feeling the nap slight differences in the height of the pile (nap) were detected, even the thinnest areas were still quite thick. But two or three years ago this fault became more prevalent and the clipping got worse, so that in one area the nap would be a full inch thick or barely thicker, and in other areas of the rug it would be only half an inch thick, and in some few areas, only one-quarter inch thick.

It was logical, therefore, that anyone buying a new rug would not accept one of these, certainly not at full price.

It became necessary for us to get down on our hands and knees and examine each one of these rugs by passing our hands over the entire field of the rug. Even then, we occasionally missed some of these areas.

Generally, these areas had a sparceness of nap as well. If it was a case of the nap being depressed by being packed down in shipment, a wet towel placed on the nap of the depressed area, and a hot iron lightly placed on top of the wet towel, immediately raised the nap. This steaming will also correct almost any crease from folding or any depressed nap where a heavy piece of furniture has stood. It is easy, and a quick, almost effortless, cure.

Why would this happen only in the city-made rugs of Hamadan, and not in the outlying districts where the Ingelas, Dargezines, and dozens of other district or village rugs that belong to the Hamadan family are woven and which are marketed in that large city?

The only sensible answer we can arrive at is, that the small children are doing much of the weaving in Hamadan which their parents formerly did. Children have always woven and helped, especially in finishing the sides. But, if you go to Hamadan today you will find thirty or forty factories that were not there a few years ago. The grown people can earn more in these factories than at the loom.

A few years ago, I recall selecting a dozen of the most attractive Kapoutarhangs I had seen, at one of the larger importing houses. I thought they were beautiful. That was when the fault was first beginning to be noticed. When the rugs arrived on my floors in Syracuse, my inspectors threw out each one–every one of these–and as much as we needed them, we shipped them back to the importer. The next time I was in his place, he took out his books and showed me where he had sold every one of them to a Boston store, and had not had one of them returned.

It should be noted that down through the years Boston has been famous for not paying much attention to irregularities, and many defects which we find people unwilling to accept, whether they live in Massachusetts, Texas, Florida or California, are readily accepted in Boston. This statement has been made to me hundreds of times by different importers.

Of course, a person buying a rug at a used rug sale will accept a rug worn thin, so why should they object to a few thin places in a new rug? The chances are these thin places will last much longer than the old thin rug.

Again, these children in clipping the pile as they weave think nothing of it if they clip one section a little shorter. I have an idea that New York importers will compel a correction on these Kasvins. Auctions and used rug sales are probably their best outlet for these.

An IMPORTANT NOTE of interest to dealers and importers concerning difference in height of pile or bad clipping: I observed in New York a small, electrically driven, hand-shearing machine used by one man which removes the high spots and evens the nap. I watched one of my close importer friends use this for the first time. It is well worth the $375.00 cost to him and should solve this problem that has plagued the trade for 2 or 3 years on Kasvins, and even some of the fine Karachi Bokharas. This importing house has sent one of these machines to their agent in Teheran.

6. LOOSE OR BLEEDING COLORS

When red or blue dye discolors the white area in a rug, most people will object. This is why you need to buy from a reliable store. If it is a fine expensive rug, they will replace it and they can also remove the stains without damage to the rug in most cases.

In the vast majority of cases it is not a question of loose dyes, but rather that of surplus dye dust being left when they water washed the rug in Iran.

If you have the *National Geographic Magazine*, dig out your January 1968 issue and turn to page 41. Here you will see how they wash the rugs, and it is little wonder that there is not more of this. In America we would not think of rolling a rug soaking wet, but only after the water had been removed. Here you will note that the rugs have been rolled while wet and one end of each rug still remains in some water before being lifted out and laid on the rocks to dry under the sun.

We usually reject a rug with these stains, and then if we still find a little discoloration when we get it to our showrooms, we do one of two things.

We take it to our cleaning plant, wash it, and thoroughly rinse the rug with hundreds of gallons of water, and then pass the rug through two large rubber rolls (wringer) to squeeze out all of the water. That usually gets rid of all the surplus dye for good and it does not reappear.

If there are very small amounts on the white and near the design, we can easily bleach these out without affecting the other colors, even though this bleach does touch the reds and blues in the design adjacent to the stains.

A very satisfactory bleach to buy is a small inexpensive package of Tintex or Rit and mix it with water as indicated in directions on the package and bring to a boil. Then, with a small brush touch the stained areas, and you will find that they quickly disappear.

7. POORLY OVERCAST SIDES AND ENDS NOT PROPERLY SECURED

This is a fault that is common with a large percentage of the rugs arriving from Iran today. The edges are so thinly overcase (about one-half as many stitches and half as much wool used in finishing sides by the simple overcasting as is necessary) that the amount of wool used does not cover the edges in many cases.

While this wrapping along the sides will not affect the life of the main part of the rug, if it is replaced in a few years, nevertheless, the retailer should see that you have a good substantial edge that you will not have to replace in fifteen to twenty years under normal usage.

The ends of most rugs are not properly secured. In most cases, the rug is sold just as it comes from Iran, and the retailer sells it as he gets it from the importer. Here is where most orientals are badly damaged by having a few lines of the end border eaten away (gradually disappearing) from traffic and vacuum cleaning over a few years. These ends should be securely fastened. Anyone can do this, and it doesn't take an expert.

Here I tread on many retail dealers' toes. They are unwilling to spend the $5.00 to $50.00 ($50.00 on a large rug) necessary to do a proper job on the four edges of the rug. We ourselves know this is a costly but very essential part of the retail selling expenses. We have at least three people in our Service Department, and 90% of their work is taking care of edges and ends of new rugs. We would not spend some $500.00 a week, or $20,000 a year, on this one item if we did not think it was very important. Forty-five years of doing this tells us it is well worth the effort and expense.

74

If you have no repairman in your town, it is a simple matter to get the right colored wool yarn and do this yourself. Add a little wool to the overcasting, and whatever method you use, secure the ends to make sure that the two or three rows of weft (or even one row if that is all there is) are sewed so that these weft lines will not pull out.

8. CHEMICALLY WASHED AND PAINTED RUGS

While this was, to my mind, the greatest risk in buying a new oriental rug from 1905 to 1955, today there is little or no risk on this point. As explained in my large book in the chapter on this subject, more than half of all the rugs imported during this fifty year period were both chemically bleached and painted.

Today, only a fraction of the Sarouks and a very few of the Dergazine runners are so treated. The cost is prohibitive and the only reason they are treated is that when some of them are lightly bleached, they have such bad hairbrushes (faded out changes of colors) that it becomes a necessity, regardless of the cost.

You may be sure these painted and chemically washed rugs would be salable in the larger cities today if they were available. Only the high labor cost in America has nearly eliminated this process.

A top executive in one of the larger stores in New York, in his letter to a doctor who bought a washed and painted Sarouk, said they approved this chemical washing and painting of oriental rugs.

Today, most of the dealers will tell you that the rug has been so treated, if you ask them.

There is a great risk in buying a used rug, and this point becomes important because there are so many of these. They have comparatively little value compared to the used rug which was untreated (in natural colors) when originally bought.

9. SALTWATER DAMAGE

There is little danger of your buying a saltwater-damaged rug today from any oriental rug store or in a large store. However, it did happen to our doctor at the Midwest clinic, and from a very large store in New York on one of their used rug sales.

Many years ago the danger was much greater, but the ships are better today, and the rugs are evidently packed better against this danger. If a shipment does get damaged by salt water, which, as we have explained, rots the area of the rug where salt water gets on it and stays during the trip, every importer carries insurance against this risk. If he has any such damage he collects from the insurance company. The insurance company generally turns it over to an auction house. In the old days most of these were sent to an auction house at 499 Broadway and certain stores, jobbers, and auction houses bought them. The Kirman rug our Mr. E bought in Atlantic City no doubt came from this source.

Any time a rug becomes rotten and is easily torn by taking in the hands and applying pressure on the back, it is due to either salt water or dry rot, and any reliable store will make good on such a rug when this is discovered, whether it be one year or five years later. You will know it in that time. A weak or small amount may not cause the rug to go to pieces immediately, but you may be sure it will generally be detected within a year.

There is no alibi that any dealer can give to relieve him of this responsibility because there is no way whatsoever that this could be caused in your home, except the following:

a. Continuous wetting of the rug, such as a potted plant seepage or leaking, over a considerable period.

b. Spillage of some acid—but where would that come from? Many years ago the acid from a radio battery was responsible once in a thousand times, but that is hardly a possibility today.

c. A great amount of dog urine, especially in the same spot, is harmful. This causes a bad stiffness and perhaps a weakening of the fiber. A few accidents are removed without damage if sponged off in time, so don't keep our wonderful canine friends who are members of the family off your oriental rugs.

10. JUFTI KNOTS

You can't do anything about this and you can not tell whether or not your rug has some of these knots. This is simply the tieing of the individual hand-tied knot in Iran, or elsewhere, by the weaver tieing the knot on four rows of warp threads instead of two. The rug is simply less compact and has less wool in it, and takes less time to weave and should cost less. Yes, it is the desire for low-priced rugs in America that has been the curse of the rug-weaving industry in Persia (Iran).

While we blame the Europeans and especially the West Germans for many of our troubles in Iran today, and also for the high prices of old

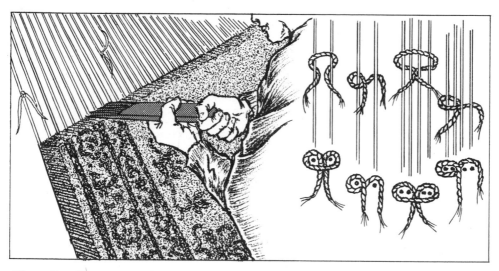

Figure 5. Knots used in oriental rugs. The left sketch, showing a loom, illustrates the reason for white knots. The ends of warp threads being tied in the field of the rug results in white knots. (See Chapter Seven, Checkpoint 13.) The sketch at the right illustrates the use of four warp threads to tie the false or jufti knot instead of the honest knot with two warp threads.

rare rugs in America, still we are indebted to them for improving the quality of many types of rugs.

They are especially fond of the rugs from the Herez District. Instead of finding great stacks of the junkiest of junky type Herez and Gorevans on the market today, you find good to superior carpets in these weaves. There is a definite improvement in the many qualities of rugs from the Herez District. You seldom see one of the burlap-type affairs that were in the New York market in great numbers a few years ago.

The rugs from the Sarouk District, at least the Sarouks, are better than a few years ago. Especially is this true of the European-type Saroku (employing the old classical designs) and the Sarabend Sarouk. These are the best Sarouks to come to America in many years. The typical Sarouk that was made, and continues to be made, for the American market in lesser numbers, the rose or red field Sarouk with the allover detached floral designs that is typical of most every one of these, shows some little improvement, but you will find very poor ones and still others much improved. The old story: Rugs by the same name vary greatly in quality.

The contract quality (best quality 80–40) Kirmans, are closely supervised and woven under contract, and the jufti knot is not an issue.

Many fine rugs like the Nain, of course, could not be so fine if they cheated and used the jufti knot.

Most of the rugs from the Khurasan (Meshed) District have used this jufti knot as their regular knot from time immemorial. The better rugs woven on the great looms in Meshed are more like Tabriz rugs. Their correct name is Turkbaff, or Turkibaff, although most dealers want to call then Ispahan. We used the name Ispahan-Meshed on these to make a line of distinction with the real Ispahan, a fine and much thinner rug.

Our big problem with the jufti knot is with the many types of rugs woven in the city of Hamadan and the nearby districts. Most of our scatter rugs, runners, and many of our carpets come from this district. There is a definite cheapening down on the majority of all the rugs that come from this great district.

The jufti knot is not used in Pakistan and Afghanistan. Germans are no doubt responsible for improvement in quality of most of the rugs being woven in Afghanistan as these rugs are also among their favorite types.

Rugs from India are no problem. They are woven, so many knots to an inch, or other standard, as specified in contracts.

Of course, when one particular type of Persian rug slips in quality, another much better type appears. Note how superior the Guenstepeh is to the well-known Kapoutarhang. This, as has been stated, is due to the modernization in the large city of Hamadan. The fact that the woman can get much more in factories, leaves much of the weaving to the children.

Most of the high plateau wool around the Hamadan District is of very excellent quality, so even less tightly woven rugs will usually last a lifetime. Of course, we would like it better if they made every rug right, but then that would eliminate a lot of people buying oriental rugs. And when you count the cost of these over a period of thirty years, the cost per year, in addition to their charm, they are far less expensive than ordinary broadloom.

I am not justifying the jufti knot, but I do say that many of the old coarser Kurdistans and other rugs without fine weave have been among the most attractive rugs made, and they were durable.

11. DEAD WOOL

Dead wool means that the wool has been taken from a butchered

78

sheep and, worse still, instead of being plucked, it was removed by the use of lye and knife to scrape it from the skin.

There is not much you can do about this because it would mean you would have to set yourself up as a judge of wool and then your hand would have to pass over every area of the rug. It is hard to detect, though there is a different feel.

The only rugs I have seen where this has happened was on a few Herez, mostly the cheapest grade, but we also had a few of the Mehriban quality of Herez go bad within a year to four years. This stopped several years ago on Herez rugs.

If you should be so unfortunate as to buy such a rug, you will find that it will wear down in one to four years, while the same rug with good wool will not be worn in thirty years. I have not seen any cases of this recently, though I am sure some dead wool finds its way into many rugs. Any dealer who uses the alibi that your electric cleaner must be too strong, or not set right, is dodging the issue. While some cleaners might be stronger than others, no electric cleaner is going to wear off the nap of a good rug in one to four years.

Again, the answer is to buy from a store that will stand back of anything it sells. Suppose you bought such a rug at auction and went back one year later, would the auctioneer replace it? I will let you answer that question. There can be no alibi by the store that receives such a complaint.

12. ORIENTAL RUGS FROM INDIA

From India are coming great numbers of handwoven oriental rugs. Over 2,000,000 people are involved in this Rug Industry in India. Most of these rugs are woven in the light pastel colors and most employ the designs of the French Aubussons and Savonneries. A very large number are made in Chinese design. Others are made in two tones, such as white and buff, white and yellow, white and green, and white and blue. Still others are made in one color, the only design being the hand-carved border and medallion.

There are many qualities in all of these designs. Today there are some seventy-five or more small companies who are making these rugs. These are in addition to the old large established companies, some of which have been in existence for over 75 years. Most of these get contracts, mainly from American importers, then buy the dyed wool, and then have the rugs woven in the many cottages to whom they furnish the paper scale patterns in color.

Each of the many companies has its own trade names for certain designs and their different qualities. Each American importer who contracts for these, either uses the Indian name on the invoice, or has his own trade name for certain designs and the different qualities. A few have registered their trade names in Washington. Oftentimes the same general designs are used by a number of companies. The best known, and at the moment the most popular of the Chinese designs, are sold under several names. There may be some minor differences in the design, and some difference in the shade of color used on the cream or ivory background. The shade of green, or blue, or red, or gold, and other colors, may vary. We call our two qualities Keen-Lung and Super Keen-Lung. But in the main there is little or no difference in the design of these rugs. One will claim that his rug is better or slightly better than the other two or three best in this design. We have been offered prices on very cheap grades in this design, but have not ordered them.

The main thing to check on buying a rug from India, after you find the colors and designs you like, is to make sure that it has 100% wool nap. Practically all of these will have the 100% wool pile, and the tag on the rug *must* indicate that, as it is required by the government. But if you are looking for a fairly good rug at a very low price, even one of these rugs with 70% wool and 30% jute will be a good buy. Imagine one of these handwoven rugs at $195.00 to $250.00 for a 9 × 12 ft. size.

For many years we did carry a limited number of these with some jute in them and they have proven to be satisfactory. In fact, I don't recall any one of these going bad over the many years.

I recall many of the rugs used at the Lake Placid Club with 100% jute and no wool lasting there for over 20 years. The lowest quality you can buy today will have 70% wool. But this question of some jute is no problem, because with the 100% wool rug costing only an extra $25.00 for a 9 × 12 ft. size more than the one with 30% jute, few, if any, of these without 100% wool will be imported. And, again, the tag will indicate what the nap is—a must by government regulations.

In buying one of the best or least expensive of these, you have to do very little checking. Some few will be slightly irregular to the extent that they will vary an inch to three inches in width for a 9 × 12 ft. rug, but that is seldom the case. Some few will have a fullness, causing the rug to buckle a little. This is readily corrected by sizing the rug.

Some few will have a little uneven clipping, but this it not serious and will seldom be noticed even on your floors.

When one shows a ridge or crease from being packed for shipment in large bales from India, this is readily eliminated by placing a damp cloth over the area and ironing, or using a steam iron on the area. One stroke of ironing over this crease immediately raises the nap.

SO ACTUALLY THE ONLY REAL PROBLEM YOU HAVE WITH ONE OF THE NEW RUGS FROM INDIA IS GETTING THE DESIRED COLORS AND DESIGN, AND MOST IMPORTANT, THE RIGHT PRICE. It is not too difficult to compare quality, values, and prices at different dealers.

OUR PRICE LIST WILL HELP YOU A GREAT DEAL ON THIS. Read our Chapter Eight, on "CHANGES SINCE PUBLICATION OF MY LARGE BOOK." Also our Chapter Nine on "OUTLOOK FOR THE FUTURE ON ORIENTAL RUGS."

Instructions for cleaning these rugs are given in our Chapter Eleven on "CARE OF ORIENTAL RUGS."

13. PRICES

I am not going to try to give you any definite price to pay for any particular name rug. Too many factors enter. Only one writer has ever tried to lay down prices to pay for different types of rugs, and he gave general prices per square foot. That was my old, dear friend, Dr. G. Grifin Lewis of Syracuse, who did this over fifty years ago. He soon found that this was his worst mistake, and I recall that when I later helped him revise his book, he was glad to omit all mention of prices.

Perhaps a little general discussion will be of some help to you. We have written a thousand times that rugs by the same name vary greatly as to value. They vary as to fineness of weave (the finer rug taking more time to weave, hence costing more as a new rug); they vary as to the quality of wool used, and the combination of colors or the total beauty of the rug. All the points we have discussed enter to some degree in the value of the individual rug.

We are talking about *new* oriental rugs, and it follows that it takes much longer to weave a fine Nain than to weave most fine Kashans, Qums, Kirmans, Ispahans, Sarouks, and other fine rugs.

For me to try to tell you what you should pay for each type of rug in the different sizes would be most unfair, as I would be trying to lay down the margin of profit that the dealers in different localities should charge. And, as we say repeatedly, rugs by the same name vary greatly as to quality, beauty, and price. Some dealer may buy to better advantage than another, and the gross mark-up varies widely. Some of us try to sell for 33% to 40% while many stores feel that 60% is a necessary margin. Such mark-up is, as a rule, not going to give the dealer a net profit of more than 5% to 10%.

Of course, there are many cases of ridiculously large mark-ups on rugs. I called your attention to two sales, one held in Coral Gables, Florida, and one in Savannah, Georgia. A Bokhara was listed in each instance, in a 10×14 ft. size, as being a $4000.00 value at regular price, and it had been marked down to $2000.00. At $2000.00 they were asking more than twice the cost of the rug. These, of course, were sales by itinerant dealers, one of which was held in an old established department store.

Now, those same sales had some right values, or rugs that seemed to be priced from 40% to 100%. I could sit here and write a thousand pages on the subject of price, and it might help you a little.

A little common sense by the prospective buyer on the prices of certain types in certain general sizes, such as 9×12 ft., should give you a pretty good idea of what you should pay for new rugs of the different types.

Again, as I have said, I do not want to sit in judgment on the prices other dealers have charged you.

About all we can do to help you on this point is to send you our latest price lists upon your request, and in this we give you a rather good range of prices for new rugs of different types and different sizes. Check these with your local dealer if you are looking at his rugs and it will give you a general idea of what you should pay.

I included prices as a check point only because we get many letters with colored pictures of rugs from people all over the world who have bought oriental rugs, and they want us to tell them if they have made a good buy.

In the first place, even though the colored picture of a rug will generally tell the name, it will not tell us whether it is one of the best of that type. Only seeing and taking the rug in hand will tell us that. To those who write us in the future for such information, I will be inclined to decline their request. If they have inherited a rug or owned it for many years, we will try to tell them what we can about the rug.

It is not too difficult to learn the approximate price you should pay for a NEW oriental rug. It is more difficult to know what price is right for an antique, semi-antique, or those we class as used rugs. Even though new rugs vary as to quality and beauty, the difference between the choicest of the type and a lesser quality of the same is not difficult to ascertain with a little effort.

You should expect to pay more for a Nain rug from Iran than any other new oriental. The best of these have some 500 to 600 hand-tied knots to the square inch, and most of those we have had recently in the approximate 3×5 and 5×8 ft. size, have had over 600 knots to the square inch.

Using two sizes, like the approximate 4×6 ft. rug and the 9×12 ft. carpet, for some general comparisons, and then letting you approximate the cost of other sizes on a square foot basis for cost or selling prices, we will present a few generalizations.

You will pay more for the good, contract-quality Kirman, Kashan, Ispahan, Qum, Sarouk, and best Tabriz than for most others. The best quality Kirmans should not vary too much, not over $200.00 at most; but they will at some dealers.

Many Kashans vary greatly as to quality and beauty and price. One may cost twice as much as the other in the same size. The Qum (or Ghoum) is approximately the same price as the Kashan. Tabriz rugs vary greatly in quality. One may be as fine as a Kashan, and the other can be very coarse, ugly, and cheap. The average is between these two.

The Ispahan should be very fine and quite thin. Some of these come with very poor wool, but a good one is a great rug. Not many in the 9×12 ft. size are available. Do not confuse the real Ispahan with the Turkbaff rug that most dealers insist on calling Ispahan. See my large book for full details.

There are three different types of Sarouks coming in today and they should not vary over $50.00 for the 4×6 ft. size, nor more than $150.00 for the 9×12 ft. size. And yet, a few days ago, in a city here in Florida, I saw a bright, average, good (not one of the best of its type) Sarouk, a Sarabend Sarouk, for which the buyer had just paid $1250.00. A few hundred dollars too much at this time. For more details on Sarouks see Chapter Eight, "Changes Since Publication of My Large Book" (in 1962).

Some of the best Joshigans and a few others will be nearly as fine.

Now, I have not intended giving the impression that fineness of weave means everything to me when actually I like some of the less finely woven rugs to live with.

Do not be guided by exaggerated advertisements. Any time anyone advertises a rug at half price, which should mean that he is selling at less than cost, you should be wary. Either the rugs have something very wrong with them, or he is lying; and it is ten to one the latter case.

Rank misstatements are often the rule at an auction. Near Syracuse, the auctioneer said the Kirman was worth $4000.00, and someone actually bid up to $1500.00 for it. He could have bought the top grade Kirman from us or another good store for somewhat less and have some one to depend on for years, rather than buying it from an itinerant.

I wish I could help more as to prices you should pay. If I should give present minimum and maximum prices for each type, my book would likely be out of date on this in a few years.

Check at a couple of good stores. Our best help to you is to offer to send you our descriptive list with prices, which you will find a very good guide and will be more up-to-date than anything we can tell you in this discussion on prices.

Always keep in mind that rugs of the same name vary as to quality, beauty of design, harmony, and combination of colors. Do not pay too much more than our list price and you will be pretty safe. Additional information on prices is given in Chapter Twelve.

14. IS THE RUG A REAL HANDMADE ORIENTAL RUG OR IS IT A MACHINE-MADE COPY OR IMITATION?

Many machine-made rugs loomed in the United States copy oriental designs. Many machine-made rugs imported from Belgium, France, England, and Italy, also copy or imitate oriental rug designs. Some are very good quality and some are junk.

This discussion may seem unnecessary to anyone who has lived with the real oriental rug. It has always amazed me how anyone with the least bit of judgment could fail to see or note the difference between a machine-made copy and the real oriental rug. I suppose the same person might not see the difference between a $1.00 print of a famous Rembrandt painting in a store, and the real painting worth $300,000.00.

Right off I can tell you that the buyer of the oriental rug copy will never realize much from the sale of his rug. Nor can he trade it in. If he sells it a few months after purchasing it, he will be fortunate to get one-half his purchase price.

The real oriental rug has good value, usually increasing in value over the years.

But the fact is that a number of people will bring some of these copies in (generally they have inherited them) and want to know what they are worth, thinking they are real oriental rugs.

I am sure that anyone who has lived with oriental rugs can immediately tell with one glance whether or not it is a real oriental rug. But if you come up with such a good copy and are in doubt, then you can

Figure 6. Ad of a well-known department store advertising machine-made rugs from Belgium.

tell by opening the nap and seeing the loop of the knot at the base of the nap where it is tied around the loop strings. We show a drawing of the knots in Figure 5, in check point No. 10 of this chapter.

The copies or imitations are no competition to the real oriental rug. They only compete with other machine-made rugs. Actually, it is a compliment that these rugs want to copy orientals. That makes the real thing more desirable.

BUT IT DOES MAKE ONE WONDER WHAT HAS HAPPENED TO THE RELIABILITY OF MANY GREAT NAME STORES.

ON THE PRECEDING PAGE IS A BEAUTIFUL AD OF A LARGE WELL-KNOWN DEPARTMENT STORE.

I have seen similar ads in New York stores, but not quite as misleading. The ad appeared December 15, 1968, and we have reproduced all details except actual pictures of three rugs, and have omitted NAME OF STORE.

But many such ads have been used by OTHER STORES. Stores in my own hometown have advertised these; but not so misleading.

They say "FABULOUS IMPORTED ORIENTAL DESIGN RUGS." What do they mean by the word "Fabulous" when they apply it to an inexpensive machine-made copy? It can't be fabulous by reason of a scoop by this store as dozens of other stores have imported these same rugs from Belgium. Nor can the word "fabulous" refer to price because at least one New York store has advertised these for much less. They can't mean "fabulous" by reason of being made in Belgium, as they are not as good in quality, or as to likeness in design, as some of the American machine-made copies, such as the Karastan. Are they "fabulous" because union labor is a little cheaper in Belgium?

NOW, THE REAL COMPLAINT I have against such an ad is that it is hoped that many people will fall for the words: "FABULOUS IMPORTED ORIENTAL———" and will think they are real oriental rugs. I certainly would discount any statement in any other ad by that store on other articles if I lived in that city where this ad appeared.

The Oriental Rug Association in New York City would do well to call this ad and other similar ads to the attention of the Federal Trade Commission in Washington.

Alongside each of three rugs pictured, they simply had the name Sarouk beside one, Kirman beside another, and Kashan beside the third. They did not say Sarouk *design,* and the same with the Kirman and Kashan. Of course, this large store does not have a regular oriental rug department. Such ads perhaps explain why many large stores are also willing to put in print rank exaggerations about their used oriental rug sales.

If you have been in business 45 years, as I have, you know that you do not build a great reputation on such ads. You may make volume sales temporarily, but you do not fool the public continuously.

ORIENTALS HAND-WOVEN IN AMERICA?

It is surprising how many people have asked the question or made the statement to the effect that they understood some of these rugs are being woven in New Jersey or Long Island. I presume their basis for such a statement is that they know that thousands of rugs go to the two (and the only two) plants that do the chemical washing of many rugs that come to America.

The absurdity of such a statement is so evident. One does not have to be a good mathematician to estimate what the cost of a rug made by child labor at 5 to 15 rials per day (15¢ to 45¢ a day in American money) would be, and for the finest master weavers on Kirmans at the highest rug-weaving salary of 35 rials, or about $1.00 a day.

Few women in American make less than $10.00 a day. Compare this with the 15¢ to 45¢ a day, and it is plain to see that any rug that now costs $100.00 from Iran would cost at least 30 times that, or $3000.00. The finest Kirman would cost ten times as much—the $1000.00 Kirman costing $10,000.00. To be sure, any number of people could learn to weave quite readily, but it is the difference in the stand-ard of living that makes such a statement incredible.

In our Chapter Eight we point out that these wages are being changed rapidly in Iran, and you can look for sharp increases each year as the industrialization in Iran proceeds at a rampant pace.

CONFUSION JUSTIFIED

Even though people who have had an interest in oriental rugs and made a little study are not easily fooled by misleading ads, in spite of what I have said I can understand some of the confusion. Magazines publish articles on oriental rugs and seldom is there one that is of much help to the public. This very day, as I close this subject, an article in *Town & Country*, February 1969 issue, comes to my attention. It devotes four pages to rugs. A double page with this heading:

ANTIQUE RUGS

EYE ON LIVING

BLUE-CHIP INVESTMENT

and some pictures of very rare rugs. It refers to some of the rarest old Aubussons and Savonneries, and Persians such as Kashans and Ispahans, and adds, "Unlike bonds and mortages and title deeds, you can form a personal attachment to your investment in antique rugs." It then lists the companies that furnish these rugs (possibly a paid advertisement). I applauded and rejoiced at this fine publicity and display of choice rugs.

I then turned the page, and the heading was:

EYE ON LIVING
THE MODERN RUG MARKET

I quote the first two paragraphs. "The idea that a modern rug makes a snug investment may come as something of a surprise. When you stop to consider its attributes, however, it begins to look as attractive as Xerox in 1950.

"We speak now not of common, everyday, wall-to-wall flowers but of rugs that command the respect of collectors and connoisseurs for tremendous artistry in design as well as execution. Quite a number of real masterpieces are being produced today and while they lack the antiques' distinction of age, they don't have the moth holes either."

And then follows this paragraph.

"Availability is one of the things in favor of the new rug. To find a really marvelous one, you don't have to bargain in a dusty bazaar in Marrakesh or spend precious time haunting auctions and estate sales. You simply saunter into a well-lit showroom or department store and take your pick. Knowledgeable rug investors frequently mention Karastan, Bigelow and Cabin Crafts as manufacturers of quite exciting designs." And I omit the names of the dealers that are referred to.

Then follows another small paragraph.

"Who knows? Your rug, loomed today, could become that magic carpet—tomorrow's priceless heirloom."

With all due respect to these great domestic companies, Karastan, Bigelow, and Cabin Craft, who, in my opinion, have produced better rugs than the copies of orientals that come from Belgium, Holland, and other countries, no criticism of anything is intended here. But would not the writer of this article and the magazine (intentionally or unintentionally) confuse anyone who read the article except the people who know oriental rugs? Little wonder that people need to be alerted on this point.

When all is said and done, machine-made is never like the real thing.

One last word. If you look at the design in the field or in the border—any one particular design—in a machine-made rug it is exactly the same. There is no slight irregularity and it takes on a "set," or, what I call a definite machine-made look. Now take any oriental, for instance the turtle design in the border or the Shah Abbas design, and compare one turtle with another a foot away from it and you will find no two exactly alike. This is the mark of distinction of a real handmade oriental rug.

Chapter Seven

DETAILED DISCUSSION OF CHECK POINTS IN BUYING A USED ORIENTAL RUG

I cannot hope to arm you completely against pitfalls in buying a used oriental rug because I, myself, and my assistants, make many mistakes. The best we can do is to tell you the things for which you should check.

BRIEFLY, THE CONDITION AND THE PRICE ARE THE TWO DECISIVE FACTORS. Condition, type, and rarity of the rug, should determine the price.

The greatest risk in buying a used rug is paying several times more than the rug is worth. Always keep in mind that a used rug from Iran, Caucasia, Turkey, or Central Asia, in top condition is worth more, as a general rule, than the new rug of the same type. I did not include the rugs from India or China because, while these will always have some value and usually good value, their value after two, ten, or twenty years' use in America generally is less than the price of a new rug of the same type. We will discuss these later under separate headings.

Every oriental rug that has a pleasing appearance to the eye has some value no matter how worn it is. But always remember that the more perfect the used rug, the more valuable. Where some people get the idea that a badly worn rug is valuable is beyond good common sense.

OUR DETAILED DISCUSSION WILL TRY TO HELP YOU IN LOOKING FOR CERTAIN HIDDEN FAULTS THAT DO NOT READILY APPEAR IN A CASUAL INSPECTION OF THE USED ORIENTAL RUG.

WE HAVE ALREADY POINTED OUT in our chapter on "USED RUG SALES," that there is a great difference in where you buy your used rug. When you buy from a "USED RUG SALE" you will generally find that the glaring defects have been camouflaged. If you are buying from a private sale in a home or from a dealer who has taken the rug in exchange, the faults will be more easily seen and appraised.

1. WHAT IS THE CONDITION OF THE RUG?

A used rug in good condition is, as a rule, to be preferred to a new rug of the same type and quality. There are some exceptions. For example, a chemically washed and painted Sarouk, or any other type so treated, is not worth as much as any new Sarouk. This is discussed in detail under check point No. 6 on page 109.

While a little care in closely examining the rug should usually tell you its condition, we find that very few people exercise good judgment in examining old rugs. We, ourselves, have made many costly mistakes in inspecting rugs in the home or at a dealer's showroom, and have found defects once they are on our floors in our store and our critical assistants have gone over them.

As a rule, we insist on bringing the rug into our showrooms and examining it there before giving a definite price that we will pay for the rug, and the amount we will allow in exchange on other rugs.

A. Does It Have a Good Nap

First, determine if the rug has most of its original nap before checking for other defects. It is necessary to get right down on the rug and pass your hand over the rug, foot by foot, because it may be thick or have a good nap in most areas, but be worn down thin in the center or where feet have rested in front of the davenport, or, in the middle of a rug that had been used for many years in the dining room. Of course, if you are buying from a reliable dealer who permits the rug to be examined in your home, and will send it on approval for trial before buying, or if you have charged the rug in a reliable store and can return it after you get it home, then, of course, you do not need to make this minute inspection in the store. But can you rely on the salesman's statement as to thickness and thinness, and condition before you get it in your home?

I cannot tell you in detail how thick you should expect to find a used rug, but a little judgment tells you that a coarse rug should be thicker than a finely woven rug. You know that the thick nap Persian rugs are the Kasvins, the Sarouks, the Herez, Gorevans, Bijars, Ingelas, Bibika-bad, and most every type of the Hamadan family. Also, the best new pastel Kirmans are thick rugs, while the early Kirmans were more finely woven and had a short nap.

You may find that even the thick rug has considerable moth dam-

Plate 18. ANTIQUE BELOOCHISTAN from Iran, with the Mina Khani design. One of the best of the Beloochistans, but never one of the most expensive rugs even if a collector's item. A rather worn one will be worth only a few dollars, while an old thin Caucasian would be worth several times as much, and a worn rare Turkish prayer rug about twenty times as much. A collector would want only one of the best.

Plate 19. ANTIQUE PRAYER BERGAMO from Turkey (Anatolian). A collector's item, rare fifty years ago. Not made since the turn of the century. Even though worn thin it would still be a collector's item. This example is considered to be in excellent condition. Not to be found at auctions or used rug sales. Size approx. 3.5 × 4 feet. *(Courtesy of Dr. George W. Scott, Lancaster, Pa.)*

Plate 20. ANTIQUE BAKU from Caucasia. This rare type, like other good Caucasian rugs, no longer available in the market. This one is in excellent condition, but even though it were thin it would still be a collector's item and valuable. Do not expect ever to find one of these at a used rug sale. Size 3.7 × 4.9 feet. *(Courtesy of Dr. George W. Scott, Lancaster, Pa.)* ·

age, or the edges may be in such bad condition that it will cost too much to fix these to make the rug a good buy. The thick rug may be very crooked; it may have loose colors; it may have been badly repaired; it may have been cut and reduced in size; or, it may have tender, weak spots, or even bad stains.

IT IS NOT QUITE AS DIFFICULT AS IT SOUNDS TO CHECK OUT ALL THESE POINTS, AS MANY OF THEM WILL BE APPARENT IN A FEW SECONDS.

If the rug is a rare one, and has a good nap, it likely is well worth spending a good sum in having it properly renovated.

B. Is the Rug Slightly Thin?

You need not reject a thin used rug, so long as it has some nap and is not threadbare. You should pay somewhat less for it than for the full-nap rug of the same type.

C. Is It Badly Worn or Threadbare?

YOU MUST BE VERY CAUTIOUS. An average or coarse rug so worn is usually worth very little. Too often the cost of fixing the edges and ends will cost more than the old worn-out rug is worth. And nothing can be done to an ordinary old rug that is threadbare. It is never possible to replace the nap except in very small areas. Cost would be prohibitive. Such a rug with holes, worn wrinkles, and other defects would cost more to make passable than the rug will sell for after the work is done.

Such rugs as the average Hamadan, Lillihan, Afshar, Mahal, Sultanabad, Muskabad, Gorevan, Herez, Meshed, Khorassan, Bazaar Kirman, and others, when badly worn, are, as a rule, not worth repairing.

Some of the best of the old Sennas, Feraghans, Bijars, Kirmans, Ispahans, Tabriz, Kashans, Shiraz, and others, can often be renovated at a sizable cost and the expenditure will be justified.

Some of the coarser rugs like the Kazaks, Geunge, and Carabaughs from Caucasia, as well as all the finely woven rugs from Caucasia, like Daghestan, Kabistan, Shirvan, Chichi, and all of these in this family, are in such demand and bring such prices that if one can be made presentable the expenditure is justified.

However, I must add that I would not consider any of these badly

Plate 21. ANTIQUE SAROUK from Iran, approximately seventy-five years old, worn very thin and worth only about $100. If not in good condition it would be worth only one-fourth this amount. Obviously, it is impossible to appraise rugs from pictures.

worn specimens from Caucasia a good buy at anything but a low price. Europeans have made New York jobbers (small dealers operating entirely on rugs they get from estates and homes) completely unbalanced as to their worth. The intrinsic value is simply not there, regardless of the demand, unless the rug is in fair condition. Only the rarest quality of a coarse type rug is worth much money, and then only to a museum or collector.

Of course, you would not expect to find a rare, old PRAYER TURKISH RUG, such as Ghiordes, Ladik, Melez, Bergamo or Kulah, in anything but a thin condition, as a rule, and they are so rare that any one in passable condition will be valuable to any of many collectors.

I like to cherish the thought that some of the many of these we have furnished to different collectors, from 1924 down through the years, are still in good condition and have been carefully preserved. Even 45 years ago one of these appeared only in the dispersal of a collection or closing of an estate. Turkey was stripped of these rare pieces before World War I with the exception of a few Melez, Bergamos, Mudjars,

97

etc., but never a Ghiordes, Ladik, Kulah, or a few others, came from Turkey or was imported to America in all my years.

D. Has the Background Been Touched up with Dye or Ink to Conceal Worn-out Places?

I could write a book on this subject alone and if you are buying a used rug anywhere, except from a most reliable dealer whom you know will tell you all the facts, then TAKE CAREFUL NOTICE OF THIS POINT—THE WORST PRACTICE, THE LOWEST TRICK ANY STORE OR DEALER CAN PLAY ON AN UNSUSPECTING BUYER.

A very large percentage of the old rugs offered on used rug sales are so worn that they would not be salable at any price, except for the fact that jobbers or small wholesale dealers have the backgrounds painted in, in order to give the rug a salable appearance. How many hundreds of people have bought these on a used rug sale—only to find that they were completely worn out.

Only last week as I went from one importing house to another in the market, I passed small room after small room of these jobbers, and in dozens of places I saw the same thing: people sliding the rugs over their tables and dabbing ink or dye on them. Whatever they used was for the same purpose—to make a worn-out rug look better, to hide its worn-out condition, and to make it salable.

Perhaps many of the buyers are happy with their purchases for a time and do not discover this until a few years later. Many such rugs have been brought to us and when we point out the bare warp which has been dyed, they say naively that they never knew this.

One could write a book on this subject of painting in the color on these badly worn rugs. Do not mistake this, if you are a beginner, with our discussion of the chemical washing and painting of new rugs.

I have to admit that this touching up of a badly worn rug and painting in the colors, often makes it quite presentable. If you owned such a rug that looked very worn, we might recommend that you have this done at a nominal cost. You would probably think that it looked much better, and this touching up might last for ten years.

The touching up of white knots is a good practice on a rug you own. See our check point no. 13 in this chapter which covers this point on Persians and others as well as Chinese. It is discussed there. These white knots are more objectionable in old Chinese rugs.

98

THE CRUX OF ALL THIS IS NOT THAT THESE RUGS ARE TOUCHED UP and made more presentable, and then turned over to one of these stores on consignment for a used rug sale, but that generally the price asked is out of line. Too often one pays $500.00 for such a worn rug that might have been all right to buy for $100.00 for the 9 × 12 ft. size.

So, a very important point in all this is, "What should the price be on such a worn rug, or on any used rug?"

I CANNOT HELP YOU VERY MUCH AS TO A SPECIFIC PRICE. I CAN ONLY ALERT YOU TO USE SOME GOOD COMMON SENSE. My discussion on prices will add something, but this can never be spelled out in definite prices.

2. EXAMINE SIDES AND ENDS
A. Do Sides Need New Overcasting?
B. Are Ends Loose and a Part of Border or Corners Already Missing?

Having determined the thickness, thinness or worn-out condition of the used rug you are considering buying, it then is important that you examine carefully the sides and ends, to see if that wool wrapping on the sides is worn off and exposes the bare edge of the rug. Usually the ends are not properly bound, and are loose. Oftentimes, a few lines of the nap have been eaten away over the years so that part of the outer border at the ends is missing.

There is no excuse for this ever happening if the dealer who originally sold the rug had properly overcast the ends, and if the owner over the years had given the rug a little care. Most dealers sell their rugs just as they come from Iran and do not properly service them. A least bit of work, especially on the ends and sides, is required on most new rugs.

Remember, the owner of these rugs over the years has been remiss and not taken care of them if they are in this condition. The edges and ends do not wear off overnight. A bad, unfastened end does not ravel out quickly—not even in a year. When a rug is in this condition you can be pretty sure that the owners did not have it serviced in some 20 years. They spent considerable money in painting their home every few years, but they didn't take the same care of their rugs. They may have sent them to some fourth-rate cleaning plant which had no repair service. In doing this perhaps they thought they had done right by their rugs.

I have always been glad to note that the rugs which we sold some 20 to 45 years ago, when coming into our store for cleaning or trading or selling, are in very good to perfect condition and require very little work. The exceptions have been the very few cases where the rugs were not sent in for cleaning and servicing over the 20 years. There are not many such cases, but a few come to light each year.

Edges and ends can be nicely repaired or restored, but you should know about the cost. You can spend $20.00 to $50.00 on a medium size rug to refinish all four sides. The cost depends on the fineness of the rug and whether it requires a very fine wrapping, or an ordinary medium one that would take half the time.

Frequently it becomes necessary to cut away the narrow outer border and re-wrap the edges and to fringe out this narrow border on each end and firmly secure the ends. This is better than having the rug (whose outer border may be eaten away) so badly repaired that the work done on it does not improve the looks very much.

As a rule, we prefer the loss of a small outer border to a badly repaired one.

IN THE CASE OF A VERY RARE AND VALUABLE RUG, THE CORNER CAN BE RE-WOVEN. But unless the weaver has some old wool yarn from the back of an old saddlebag, this corner with the new wool will fade out to a lighter shade in a few years.

So, it is most important to determine if the rug, for example, one about 4×7 ft. at $50.00, is a good value. Unless you have an idea of the cost of repair and the value of the rug after being repaired, you should not buy it.

You need to know whether it is just an average rug, or a poor quality rug, or if it is a chemically washed old rug, or a very good rug, or a rare rug. If it is a real rare rug, it may justify spending a good sum to restore it.

Sure, it is fun to gamble if the price is low, and you will not be hurt much if your $50.00 or $100.00 rug proves to be worthless.

C. Are Edges Curled Under?

This occurs mostly in finely woven rugs. We listed this as a fault to check on when buying the new finely woven rugs. Most of the old rugs that show up with their edges curled under were that way when they were purchased and have remained that way for the 10, 20, or 50 years they have been in use.

So many of the old, finely woven rugs, especially old Sarouks,

Kashans, Kirmans and many others, will have this bad defect. After having been used for many years with the edges (sides) curled under, when the edge is forced out flat, there will be a real ditch worn in the nap. The very edge of the rug, which should have been flat, with the wool wrapping or overcasting protecting the edge, now has the middle or outer part of the outer narrow border as the edge. This edge is now, as a rule, worn right down thin to the warp, and as stated, when flattened out or forced out, there is a regular ditch or worn lines.

It is too late to stretch this out or to make these curled edges flat by sewing or ironing out, as this is so confirmed that nothing will correct it or make the rug lie flat. The only solution is cutting away part of the outer border (better to remove the entire outer narrow border and refinish the side).

This does not just happen in the original purchaser's home. The edges were curled when they bought the rug. Any reliable dealer would never have let this get by, and it is incredible that so many people buy a fine rug and do not even notice this down through the years. SURELY THEY MUST HAVE BOUGHT THIS AT AN AUCTION, OR FROM SOME FLY-BY-NIGHT ITINERANT DEALER.

In all my 46 years in the business, I HAVE NEVER FOUND ONE WHO DID NOT NOTICE EVEN A SLIGHT CURLING UNDER when buying the rug from us. Customers invariably see the smallest faults that our salesmen and service department fail to detect. These show up better in your home than they do in the store.

Again, this old rug need not be rejected if the rest of the rug is good, or if the other faults are not too serious. It will cost a good sum to correct this but a good rug will justify the expense. A badly worn rug, even though finely woven, will often not justify the expense to correct this.

3. HAS THE RUG HAD CONSIDERABLE REPAIR?

Excellent repair work, such as reweaving or repair of holes or moth-eaten places, does not hurt an old rug to any great degree. This means the repaired places do not show from the nap side, and they do not stand out when you examine the underside of the rug. Frequently, when an old rug has been repaired, these sections will stand out by reason of having been done with new wool that matched the nap when the work was done, but after a few years' use the new wool mellowed or faded to a lighter shade causing these repaired areas to stand out and spoil the appearance of the rug. This could have been avoided if the repairman had woven the area with old wool or aged wool. The only way this is obtained is from the back of an old saddlebag, where the wool will have faded, or where some enterprising repairman has been resourceful enough to have exposed wool to the sun. Even so, when he ties the knots and clips it even with the rest of the nap, it will still fade some.

If the rug is a good quality rug, and not a real rare rug, then the only solution is to tint carefully this faded-out repaired area with a fast dye, and a good ink often is the best.

If it is a very rare rug, this may still be the best solution if done by an expert, and that expert should know enough to do it gradually; that is, not try to touch it up to the exact color in the initial touching, but to improve a little and then add more later. This is in order not to overdo it or overcolor it in a quick effort.

But, of course, first see if the areas can be rewoven and what this will cost. If you examine the rug carefully, front and back, you should be able to detect repaired spots. Especially will these show up on the underside of the rug.

The worse repair places are those that have been clumsily sewed on the back and pulled together with large threads that are readily visible. The only correction for this, if it is a good rug, is to open this repaired area and re-weave it. This will be costly with today's weaving wages and the scarcity of good repair people.

Oftentimes the best solution to this is to let the repairman insert a piece (a patch) from another old rug. Any good repairman has barrels of pieces of old rugs, or worn out rugs with good sections in them and, with considerable searching, the right patch often can be found.

Only a short time ago I had to go to Geneva, New York for personal reasons, and while there I agreed to look at an old Tekke Bokhara (people in their eighties had bought many nice rugs some 40 to 60 years ago). I examined the fine Bokhara and paid them several hundred dollars for it on the spot. It was truly a lovely Bokhara and, I thought, in top condition. I did not turn it over and examine it on the underside as I should have. But I thought I would see such defects as I rolled it up to take with me. I displayed it very proudly to my top assistants, with some alibi for paying so much for this size rug, and asked, "When have you seen one as good?"

I turned the rug over to my senior repairman for minor work. In a

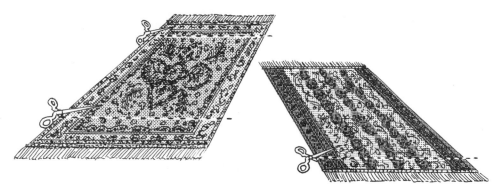

Figure 7. In checking to see if a rug has been cut down in size you look at both the nap and underside. The cut invariably will be at one end of an overall design rug or at both ends where the rug has a medallion.

few minutes he called me and showed me a very badly repaired area (not visible from the front), and also several motheaten places on the nap side.

Fortunately he was able to restore these, but only after two full days of work on this rug at the actual labor cost of $45.00. Without this perfect restoration my mistake would have been a costly one. Had I seen these in the home I would not have paid as much. After 46 years, and after having made many such costly mistakes, I should not have missed these defects. One good test is to hold the rug up to the light, with underside toward you, and you will be amazed at how many small, napless (lace-like) spots you will see.

SO NOW YOU SEE WHY WE SAY THAT IT IS SUCH A GAMBLE TO BUY A USED oriental rug without being able to examine it in your home. When you buy from a reliable store, if you discover bad defects in the rug once you have it home, it can be returned. And you can see why we insist in most cases in having the rug brought or sent to our store for examination before we make our offer to buy or exchange.

4. HAS THE RUG BEEN CUT?

You will find many oriental rugs that have, for one reason or another, been cut to reduce the size of the rug. Generally, the rug has been cut and a piece taken out in order to shorten the length of the rug. In many cases this reduction in length has been made by the owner in order to use the rug in new quarters or in another room. In many other cases the rug has been cut in order to eliminate badly worn areas (sections of rug that have become eyesores), or the rug has been cut to eliminate damage from salt water (rotten area caused by salt water in voyage to America).

In a rug with an allover design, it is necessary to cut only one piece at one end. When expertly sewed by the old best method, this is not readily detected. Only by carefully examining the pattern in the border on nap and underside can you detect this.

Seldom can the border design be absolutely perfectly matched in each design. This expert job which is difficult to detect will have been done years ago before wages of repair men and women reached the present level. To sew a rug in this manner with one or more stitches for each warp thread is very costly today. If you are considering reducing an old rug by cutting out a piece and sewing the border back on, it is often wise to do the cheap job (a simple sewing on back) which is easily detected from the underside but looks good from nap side and which is durable and strong enough to last for many years.

Now, if the rug you are considering cutting has a medallion, it will be necessary to cut the rug at both ends otherwise the medallion will be off center. So check.

An oriental rug that has been cut loses some of its value. My guess is that the value is reduced by half.

Again, I caution you that the expert job done years ago will not be readily discovered.

If you buy an expensive rug and want an expert job done you must be prepared to spend $50.00 to several hundred dollars on a 4×6 ft. size to a large carpet. So do not buy an old, beat-up rug or carpet with badly damaged sections with the idea of cutting these out and having a smaller rug left for very little money.

If you have a rug that is too large and it can be reduced to the desired size by eliminating the outer narrow border and not disturbing the wide main border, then this is the best procedure and the less expensive one to refinish the sides and ends. Some rugs have several narrow borders and the reduction is made easier by removing these up to the main border. Of course, you will leave any one of these narrow borders that can be left, and still reduce the rug to the size required.

The above procedure does not destroy the value of the rug to the extent that cutting part of the field out does, and sewing the border back on. The estimate that the value is reduced by half when the rug is cut is a general rule. I would say "reduced at least half" but in some cases even more.

104

Most important point of reducing size of oriental rugs applies to runners. Cutting a section out of the field and reducing the length to make the runner the right length for stairs is not quite as serious as cutting a rug that is used elsewhere. In the old days (up to about 1930), removing the narrow outer borders of an old runner so that it would be narrow enough to fit on the stair steps, increased the value of the runner instead of reducing it.

Practically all of the old runners made for the Persians' own use were approximately $3\frac{1}{2}$ ft. wide; but a more correct statement would be to say that they were almost invariably 3 ft. 2 inches to 4 ft. wide. Very few staircases would take this width. Up to 1930 you could buy a $13 \times 3\frac{1}{2}$ ft. runner, or a 15×3.8 ft. runner for less than you could buy the same quality and type in a rug about $4\frac{1}{2} \times 6\frac{1}{2}$ ft. I recall in the 1920s that every importing house had one to a half dozen piles of lovely old runners, and you could buy most of them for from $30.00 to $60.00. Today the same runner would be worth $100.00 to $250.00 wholesale. No cost in making these entered into the price because they were woven years before for the Persians' own use, and simply picked up from their homes and brought to the market.

A new runner of lesser quality in the narrow width, for example 2 ft. 6 inches wide, would cost more than the choice old runner. But until the mid-twenties there were comparatively few new runners. When people wanted oriental runners for their staircase, the dealer simply removed the outside borders from the old runner and refinished the sides, thus reducing the width, for example from 3 ft. 4 inches to a runner, say 2 ft. 8 inches.

I have been amazed to find that in hundreds of such cases, most owners of old runners were not aware that the narrow border had been removed.

Not every runner lent itself to this kind of operation. You may be sure that I was a party to many such operations on runners—even for my own home.

The new narrow runner being woven for the American market costs so many rial salaries a day to weave, but even at the few cents weaving wages, the cost is more than the cost of the old runners.

Last summer we sold our home. The lovely Serab runner on our stairs was a pair of these that had been sewed together and the outer border removed. I could not satisfy the purchaser of my home with any other runner. He could not believe that it had been cut and sewed together and that a border had been removed. BUT THE INTER-

ESTING POINT IS THAT THIS RUNNER HAD BEEN ON OUR STAIRCASE FOR OVER 30 YEARS, and was still in excellent condition. I truly believe that the young couple who bought this runner is going to have another 40 years' use before it is worn out.

No rug is so inexpensive per years' use on a stairway as a good oriental runner.

5. MOTH DAMAGE OR HOLES IN RUG

Even a thick rug can have its value reduced practically to that of a worthless rug. This is one of the most important checks to make in buying a used rug, regardless of where you buy it. In a home at a private sale, you have a better chance of detecting moth damage than you will have at an auction or a used rug sale. In these the damage will have been camouflaged so that it is not easily detected.

We wish to alarm you on this moth-damage danger when buying a used rug, and then we will try to calm you down and tell you that the risk of moths to any rug you buy is very small with today's insecticides and other preventives, if they are used.

Moths generally do their damage in dark areas, i. e., under the davenport, sideboards and other pieces of furniture. Also, the risk is greater on stair runners. In examining a rug in the home it is essential that you pull the rug from under all pieces of furniture and examine these areas of the rug most carefully, both on the nap side and on the underside.

On the nap side you must pass your hand over the nap where the areas have been under furniture or in very dark corners. You often find little pea-size areas where the larvae, worms, or eggs are still there. You can brush this out or roll it out with your fingers. Generally this is eaten right down to the warp, but the damage will not show up on the underside as a rule. If these small eaten areas are not extensive, and are spread over one square foot or even a slightly larger area, then the rug can be de-mothed and these eaten areas restored by re-weaving the individual knots. By restoring knot for knot, the rug is not badly hurt.

Excellent Mothproofing Materials Available

You can be certain of de-mothing the rug or the area completely with present-day insecticides. We prefer the material called SECT-O-

106

CIDE (old name was Keyspray). The company that bought out the old company changed the name. All the petroleum companies make a mothproofing solution and I am quite sure that the base of each of these is a solvent petroleum product, whether kerosene, dry-cleaning gas, or what not. I do know that dry cleaning gas, such as Renuzit and the like, will kill the eggs, larvae, etc., as well as mothproofing the rug for some time. I do not advise use of dry-cleaning gas because of the danger of fire. But if you can find a solvent that is not flammable and not dangerous, then apply it to the area where the moth damage is and you can be sure you will have completely de-mothed that area. You must soak that area thoroughly. Merely rubbing a little on the top of the nap is not sufficient. You can handle the small area, but if the moths have gotten in several places in the rug, then it becomes necessary to treat the entire rug. See our Chapter Eleven, "Care of Oriental Rugs."

Camouflaged Moth Damage

If the moths have eaten the underside of the rug in very small areas, then the same rule applies as above. Too often, when they have eaten on the underside, the areas are too extensive to be repaired. A rug that might have been worth $500.00 may have its value reduced to $50.00 or even nothing.

Where eaten areas are small, they will not be easily detected, but you will see them if you look carefully when buying the rug from a private home.

One of the lowest tricks used by the small, second-hand dealers that supply the rugs for the used rug sales, is to touch up the small moth-eaten places on the underside of the rug where the wool strand of the knot holds the rug. When the moths have cut this on the back, it is a simple matter to pull the nap out in these places from the top (nap) side of the rug. The fact that the nap is still intact on the nap side does not help the situation because in a short time the vacuuming and especially rug cleaning will loosen these strands that formed the knot, and you will have the many little places without nap.

If the area where this has been eaten is large, then the touching up is quite easily detected, as you can easily see the smear from the red, or black, or blue dye, or from all of these. There is no way to repair large areas that have been eaten on the back without very large expenditures.

You cannot restore the value of such a rug. You can take drastic measures that will make it usable and keep the nap from pulling out for many years. The back of the rug, or the areas where the moths have eaten, must be glued with Lastex or some other similar material which will harden and hold these loose strands of wool. There is very little resale value, but we have seen a number of cases where this Lastex has kept the nap intact for 30 years or more.

Moths Not a Serious Problem

NOW THAT I HAVE TOLD YOU THE HORRORS OF MOTH-DAMAGED RUGS, I wish to turn around and present a very bright picture on the small possibility of your oriental rugs ever having moths, provided you take the least bit of precaution.

I cannot tell you how to keep moths out of woolen sweaters, woolen socks, or clothes, but I can assure you that with a least bit of precaution, there is practically no danger from moths getting into your oriental rugs. Under "Care of Oriental Rugs," Chapter Eleven, we detail the easy way to mothproof your rugs.

For many years we have sprayed every rug we sell and every rug we send out on approval with this mothproofing material (originally called Keyspray—now called Sect-O-Cide). We have done this not only for mothproofing, but also by spraying the nap side and then brushing with a regular straw sweeping broom, we give the rug a very fresh look. One can spray this on a semi-soiled rug and you would be amazed at what a fresh appearance this gives the rug.

So, when we give a bright picture on the danger from moths in oriental rugs, we are basing this on our "table of experience" over the past 20 years. We estimate that we have sold some 150,000 to 200,000 oriental rugs during the past 20 years and in all that time our estimate of the number of rugs damaged by moths, among these many thousand rugs, would be less than 20. I can only recall some five, and all of these were in homes where both members of the family worked. The wife not only did not have time to clean, but was a poor housekeeper and other furnishings were not cared for.

AREN'T THE ABOVE FACTS ALMOST UNBELIEVABLE? You may well ask, "Then why do we have to make such a careful inspection for moths?" My reply is that many other people have not taken the precaution with the rugs they sell.

And I must admit that we get a good many rugs that have moth damage. Most of them are rugs that we had not sold in the first place.

Some of those we sold 25 to 40 years ago do come in with moth damage. As I recall, most such rugs with moth damage have come from homes where the owners have gotten quite old and are not able to do much cleaning themselves. I recall a few cases where one or both members had been in nursing homes and the home or apartment had been left intact for several months to a year, with the hope that they would be able to return, and the moths did their damage during this time.

If the rug is small, hold it up to the light with the underside facing toward you. You will see light in places which will not be seen from the nap side.

Yes, buy a rug loaded with moth eggs if it has not already been eaten. You may buy a large choice rug with moth damage if it can be re-woven perfectly for $100.00 to $300.00. (See our Chapter Eleven for more information.)

6. IS IT A CHEMICALLY WASHED AND PAINTED RUG?

This is a very important check point. The Sarouk which has been so treated will be worth from one-half to one-fifth as much as the natural-colored Sarouk which has aged and mellowed from use—being walked on, and being exposed to the air and sun.

If you are a beginner, right off you will ask, "What do you mean by being WASHED AND PAINTED?"

We have written so much on this subject during the past 46 years that we will not make a long story of this, but rather suggest that you read our chapter on this subject in our large book, *Oriental Rugs—A Complete Guide*. Also, my first small book published about 1931 had a chapter, "Beware of the Chemically Washed and Painted Rug." If you do not have one of these, and feel that you would like more details than we give here, write us in Syracuse, New York, for a free copy of our booklet on this subject, and other free material on the subject.

We have stated many times that more than half of all the oriental rugs imported from Persia from about 1905 to 1955 were both chemically washed and painted after they arrived in America. There are still two large plants doing this chemical washing. One was located in Jersey City and the other on Long Island. The Jersey City plant has been sold and moved to Long Island. Why would importers and dealers have their rugs chemically washed and painted? THE ANSWER IS SIMPLE. They wanted to sell oriental rugs.

You must remember that originally when oriental rugs were first brought to America in the late nineteenth century from about 1870 to 1900, they were rugs that had been made for the weavers' own homes, and they had been used in these homes before being sold to dealers nearby. These rugs had mellowed and the colors had toned down. The colors did not fade out but they took on a softness that age and age alone can give. The Persians, Turks, and others, like bright, prime colors and their colors were, as a rule, very bright for the past 300 years. Most new rugs are very bright. The reds, blues, greens, yellows are much nicer when they have mellowed, and even the white is nicer when it tones to cream.

So, when oriental rugs became so popular in America around the turn of the century, and the supply of old rugs was in short supply and especially in sizes America demanded, they began weaving rugs on a commercial basis for export. People were not accustomed to the real bright new rugs, and so the method of chemically bleaching the rug to kill the bright colors was developed. A chlorine bath or other chemicals reduced the bright reds to a pale, dull pink color—almost a dead looking color. It was now necessary to bring back some of the color and this was done by painting back in the reds, the blues, etc. Next, by applying wax or glycerine and rolling against hot wheels they produced a highly silky and glossy rug.

To the vast majority of people who did not take the time to investigate, the rug was beautiful and like velvet when new.

So from about 1905 to 1955 tens of thousands of oriental rugs, more particularly the rugs from Persia, were so treated. In fact more than half, and perhaps the percentage would be seventy-five, were so treated.

Practically every dealer in America sold them and liked them. Big stores in New York advertised beautifully washed Sarouks in so many words. Most dealers would tell you that they were so treated if you asked them, and many would tell you it did no damage. But there were some dealers who, when asked if the rug was treated, would deny it. I could relate hundreds of incidents where the purchaser wanted antique rugs and was sold a houseful of the washed and painted Sarouks. The last bad case I saw was in Fredericksburg, Virginia, in one of the loveliest new homes there. The couple had come to Syracuse and had bought a large semi-antique Kashan, and knowing that I would be in their town in a short time had urged me to stop by and see other rooms for which they wished me to furnish rugs. They had previously bought many expensive rugs. This fine gentleman and his wife deserved a better deal.

Of course, Fredericksburg is one of my favorite places because I have had the privilege of furnishing the oriental rugs for the historical homes there, i.e., Mary Washington House (George Washington's mother's home), and The Tavern (George Washington's brother's home). I had the privilege of giving the old Savonnerie from my home when we moved to a condominium, and I have been responsible for having a number of customers and friends give these homes a great many rare rugs.

Forgive me for going off on a tangent on a project where much sentiment is involved.

Going back to washed and painted rugs, I am proud to state that in all my 46 years I never sold one of these. When I started in Syracuse there were thirteen dealers and stores selling oriental rugs and, with one exception, they all sold these treated and painted rugs. They are not to be blamed too much because that is most of what was available, and many people wanted them for their silky sheen.

AND WHY WAS I SO OPPOSED TO THEM? First, it was for the same reason that anyone, and especially any collector who had taken the time to study or read the least bit, objected to them, but more especially because anyone who had lived with the old oriental rugs or even the new natural colored oriental rug would not like these artificial looking rugs. They had just that—an artificial look.

Initially I was opposed to them because my early teachers and collector friends berated them and would not consider them. I was taught that the chemical bath took off some of the nap, reducing a very thick rug to a medium thick rug. I also believe and found it true that the chemical took some of the natural oil out of the wool nap and that the rug would wear down much faster than the same rug which had not been treated.

NOW, AFTER ALL THESE YEARS THE PROOF OF THE PUDDING IS THE WIDE TABLE OF EXPERIENCE IN OBSERVING MANY THOUSANDS OF THESE CHEMICALLY TREATED RUGS AND COMPARING THEM WITH THEIR COUNTERPART IN NATURAL COLORED RUGS.

The proof is unmistakable. Thousands of natural colored rugs, whether they were originally bought as new, semi-antique, or antique, are today in most cases selling at twice to several times their initial selling price, while even the few washed and painted rugs that appear

111

in good condition seldom sell for more than half their original cost.

The average quality, and even most of the better qualities, have deteriorated as we predicted they would 46 years ago, and as I have said they would through the years in hundreds of articles.

The average Hamadan, Lillihan, Mosul, Mahal, Arak, Gorevan, Meshed, and even the Kirman, bought 25 to 45 years ago are almost without exception pretty sad-looking affairs today. They are mostly threadbare and sick looking. A Hamadan or Mosul that was so treated in the approximate size $6\frac{1}{2} \times 3\frac{1}{2}$, and which sold from $50.00 to $100.00, is seldom worth $10.00 or $15.00 today as it is threadbare. Most of these have already gone to the trash heap. But there are thousands of Hamadans in natural colors that have survived 25 to 45 years' usage and are in good to excellent condition and very salable at more than the original price. And the same is true for all the average weaves.

Most of the Kirmans of 40 years ago, and especially the carpet sizes, were in the same general colors and design as the Sarouk of that day. The backgrounds were red or blue and seldom ivory. They were both treated and painted. They in no way compared to the contract quality Kirman (80/40 quality) of today. These Kirmans of 40 years ago are almost invariably threadbare and of little value. The exceptions are those that were sold in natural colors, and even if they are slightly thin or quite thin they are salable rugs and bring good prices.

There are some good exceptions to the above. Occasionally we see Sarouks that have been both chemically washed and painted that were bought during the period 1924 to 1940, now some 25 to 40 years old, and which are in very excellent condition. These Sarouks seem to have withstood the wear and held their appearance better than any other type given the treatment. However, 9 out of 10 of these will have deteriorated both in wear and in appearance.

These treated rugs will, without exception, not prove to be the good property that the natural untreated rugs are. A definite rule is that they are worth less each year they are used, while so often the very opposite is true of the natural-colored rug whether it be antique, semi-antique, or new when purchased.

Most of the less expensive rugs in natural colors (untreated), sold 30 or 40 years ago, will be in good to excellent condition and the chances are they will sell for considerable more than the original cost. This is not a firm rule because one may have purchased old, thin rugs 30 or 40 years ago and used them in heavy traffic lanes so that they are pretty well beat up and have very little resale value.

How can one tell if the oriental rug is chemically washed and painted?

I am not sure I can give you sufficient information to educate your eyes in a few words. Fifteen minutes of explanation in our store with rugs to demonstrate the point generally will give you more definite information then pages of words.

But here are a few tests you can make that should help. Look on the underside of the rug and see if it is much lighter than the nap side. On a rug with a red, rose, or plum field, the underside will have a dull, faded, tanish rose, while the top will be in much deeper tones. A rug doesn't fade darker than the original colors, but rather it would tend to lighten up. If any changes develop you would expect the nap side to fade more than the underside. So many of these washed rugs were dyed to a plum or a rosy mulberry effect. Hardly an oriental was ever made in these colors. These colors are obtained only by the washing and painting process. If you have seen one or two such examples and had this pointed out to you, you are likely to detect and know the next one you see.

There are some few cases where the back of the rug is nearly the same color as the nap, and this is true particularly of the medium red field, but as a rule the above check will work.

Another good test is to examine the rug on the nap side. Assuming the rug to be a rose or red field with the design in blue, a careful check of the outline of the designs will show some of the blue overlapping the rose or red area. If there is white in some of the design, the paint on the edge of this will be easily discovered. But the washed and painted rug takes on a muggy look with use, while the outline of the natural-colored rug becomes more distinct.

All of this chemically washing and painting is done after the rug reaches New York. This type of treatment has never been applied in the Orient nor by the washers in London. They do lightly treat some of the rugs in the Orient, and especially in London, but the methods have been different and less harmful. The so-called water wash in Teheran or very light wash is done either with water or with a light lime or very weak chlorine solution. A small percentage of the rugs that come to the London Free Port Warehouse are sent out and are lightly treated, but never is the painting process used.

And we must remember that many rugs brought to America were only lightly treated with a light lime wash. I was very much against this when I started 46 years ago, but I have relented because I have observed that the light bleaching did very little harm from the durability point of view.

Many people have the idea that an antique rug should have the pale, faded appearance that one of these lightly treated rugs generally has after many years' use. They seek these colors believing them to be the real antique color. But they are so wrong. The rich colors in a natural colored rug, semi-antique, antique or new, do not take on a faded or real pastel look. The reds mellow some and even though still red, there is a real softness by reason of the age. All the other colors do the same, and even the white becomes much more beautiful when it ages to cream or a light tan.

I was about to say that only Americans will be concerned with the washed and painted rugs and that Europeans need not be concerned on this point. My large book, however, has had a large distribution in Europe and the world over. (Wishful thinking that perhaps this second book will also find readers everywhere.)

EUROPEANS MUST BE ON THE LOOKOUT FOR THE USED WASHED AND PAINTED RUGS. IN RECENT YEARS I HAVE SEEN HUNDREDS OF THESE BEING SHIPPED TO ITALY, FRANCE, AND SOME FEW TO ENGLAND from New York jobbers. All were used rugs.

Again, we are proud that we have never sold a one to any customer. If we take these in trade on a good sale, we immediately ship them to dealers in New York City where there is a ready market for all of these that we or any dealer over the country gets. BUT AGAIN THE PRICE FOR THE CHEMICALLY WASHED AND PAINTED RUG IS A FRACTION OF WHAT THE SAME NATURAL RUG IN CORRESPONDING QUALITY, SIZE, AND CONDITION WILL BE.

You will run into this situation many times; at least we do. When owners have a Sarouk they wish to sell or trade and you ask them if they know whether it is chemically treated, they quickly and sincerely say that the rug is not that type, that their parents bought it 40 years ago in some great-name store. The 40 years ago would mean the period 1925-35. We have to tell them that 9 out of 10 Sarouks sold in America between 1905 and 1955 were both chemically washed and painted, and that this process was at its height in the period 1922–32.

There is one other important point to remember on this subject. You may reason that ANY RUG YOU BUY FROM ONE OF THE RICHEST ESTATES WILL BE A GOOD HONEST RUG, AND

THAT IT WILL NOT BE A CHEMICALLY WASHED AND PAINTED RUG. That is a dangerous assumption. My experience is that at least 3 out of 4 of the oriental rugs from the great industrial giants' homes have been finely woven, chemically washed and painted rugs for which they paid more than if they had bought the best antiques or semi-antiques in the size available at the time of purchase. The exception would be the very few who studied rugs as art and made a collection of rare rugs.

One estate in Syracuse, perhaps the wealthiest citizen, had nothing but these fine, chemically washed and painted rugs with the exception of one approximately 6 × 9 ft. Afghan rug. Two of the richest estates from Detroit or vicinity that came our way had many rugs in each, and most of the rugs were the treated type.

Of course, in sizes and colors these were the only large rugs available in the soft silky types suitable to the decor which the decorators required. And it is a 100 to 1 bet that at that time the decorator didn't know the meaning of "a chemically washed and painted rug." Today, I think many, perhaps most decorators do know, and may I pin a medal on yours truly and suggest that they are indebted to me for this information.

The decorators' favorite rug or one of their favorite and most expensive rugs (cost is as much as most perfect old rugs) is the pastel Kirman. Ninety-nine out of 100 of these have the less objectionable light wash to tone down their new look and to give them the silky sheen or patina. This is not so objectionable as the other process of washing and painting. No Kirmans have been both treated and painted in 30 years. Under "Price" we tell you why this fine quality Kirman does not have as good a resale or trade-in value as most of the other fine rugs that are not treated at all. I am not referring to the old Laver Kirmans of 50 to 100 years ago, which are very rare and very valuable. I am talking about the light-colored, present-day Kirman that is given the very light chemical wash to take off the rough look and give it the pastel tones.

7. HAIRBRUSHES AND CHANGES OF COLOR

There is a difference between these two. Most people use the terms "hairbrush" and "change of color" as being synonymous, but I have always thought of them as being different.

How are you to tell which is which? In buying a used rug (and remember a used rug can be classed as just a used rug, or a semi-antique, or an antique), it is not too important that you definitely know the difference. Any rug of any type that has a change of color that detracts from the rug is worth less than it would be without this change.

You are going to find many slight changes of color in oriental rugs. And many of these shadings and changes of color in old rugs will definitely add to the beauty and charm of the rug, and not detract in the least from the rug or reduce its value.

I quote here as I did in my large book *Oriental Rugs—A Complete Guide,* in which I devote a chapter to this subject, from the Victoria and Albert Museum *Guide to the Collection of Carpets.* This is in London. I quote, "The beautiful harmony of colour presented by an old oriental carpet is produced, as a rule, with quite a limited number of tints. A conspicuous feature of many Eastern carpets is the irregularity of the tone, where one colour is used to any considerable extent, as in the ground. The native dyes vary much in tone, and when the supply of the particular shade is used up before the carpet is finished, more wool is dyed, or the nearest available shade is taken, and this may be more fugitive than the first, so that the contrast becomes accentuated by fading."

Yes, these changes are typical and many of these actually add to the beauty of the rug, especially in an open field. On such a field the gradual shading from light rose to rose in slightly deeper tones gives this open field an added charm.

However, we do see many changes in rugs that definitely detract from the beauty of the rug and reduce its value. So far we have talked about changes in natural-colored rugs, and we repeat we call these "changes of color."

Hairbrushes are those different shades brought about or accentuated when the rug is chemically washed. Many rugs are only lightly treated and are not painted. This is the treatment applied to present day Kirmans, and if they did not use the best dyes and the same dyes, these would show up with streaks. Seldom do you see a good quality Kirman with a hairbrush.

Many of the Sarouks that are lightly washed on Long Island do come out with very bad hairbrushes, and it is almost a necessity that these badly faded sections be painted in, and usually they go ahead and paint the entire rug. This is a very costly process today as compared to the light chemical bath. MOST OF THESE HAIR-

BRUSHES ARE OBJECTIONABLE AND DEFINITELY RE-
DUCE THE VALUE OF THE RUG. IT IS A SICKISH
LOOKING FADING OUT, AND ONCE YOU HAVE SEEN A
FEW YOU WILL HAVE NO TROUBLE TELLING THE
DIFFERENCE BETWEEN A NATURAL CHANGE OF COLOR
IN THE RUG AND THE HAIRBRUSH CAUSED BY THE
CHEMICAL BLEACHING.

8. STRAIGHT OR CROOKED?
IS THE RUG TOO IRREGULAR IN SHAPE?

You will seldom find an old rug perfectly straight. You have only
to look at the plates in any rug book or the rare rugs in any museum
to learn that most every one of these will have some slight irregularity
in shape. These irregularites are not objected to in an old rug as much
as they are in a new rug.

Nevertheless, I still maintain that a very badly misshapen rug loses
some of its value, and this holds even for the very rare rugs but to
a lesser extent than for the mediocre rug.

Suggest you read our discussion of this subject in Chapter Six,
"Detailed Discussion of Check List for Buying New Oriental Rugs."

9. DOES THE RUG LIE FLAT OR
ARE THERE CONFIRMED WRINKLES?

We told you in discussing new rugs that did not lie flat that they
could, as a rule, be sized and thus stretched out flat. This is a procedure
where we turn the rug upside down and fasten the rug to the floor with
brads or tacks, after pulling it out flat and taut either with a kick of the
heel or with a stretcher (a metal tool made for pulling the rug out flat
before tacking), and then wetting the rug down with a solution of cold
water glue dissolved in water. This is done best from a sprinkling can
and then swept out evenly on the back of the rug with an ordinary
straw broom—the regular household broom.

An old rug that doesn't lie flat should be sized in the same manner
and the rug pulled out until all the wrinkles are out. Even if it means
pulling the rug a little out of shape, i. e., a little wider on one end
than the other, it is better that the rug be flat.

Sometimes if these wrinkles have become so confirmed that the
ridge caused by the wrinkle has the nap worn off, then you are faced

Plate 22. ANTIQUE KHIVA BOKHARA from Afghanistan. The color and design mark this as one of the real old ones and one of the best of its type. On first viewing it would appear excellent, but closer scrutiny would reveal bad ridges with the nap completely worn off due to the fact that the rug has not laid flat for many years. Only remedy is to cut out these wrinkles and worn areas. Even then, however, it would not be considered valuable inasmuch as one end is worn quite thin.

with filling these in by weaving or just leaving the depressions there. In some cases it is better judgment to cut these wrinkled areas, and remove the wrinkle and eliminate these worn areas. Sometimes this will be a small triangle piece cut out along the side of the rug and will include one to several rows of knots. After doing this, the rug should then be sized and placed on a rubber pad or non-skid material.

10. LOOSE OR BLEEDING COLORS

You have read our discussion of this in Chapter Six on "New Rugs." Loose or bleeding colors (red or blue dyes) have stained the adjoining white nap. These can, as a rule be readily removed from a new rug.

We can generally remove the red stains on the white nap of an old rug, but the blues and greens are not easily removed.

Small stains on an ordinary used oriental rug that is intended for floor use will hardly be noticeable in a figured rug. They will be noticed in one of the plainer rugs from India, or a Kirman with open field. A bad stain on any rug naturally takes away much of the value of the rug, unless it is small enough to be pulled out and re-woven knot for knot.

Some collectors will accept old rugs with stains if the rug is a rare example and if the price is right. For my part, and if I were making a new collection for my personal use, only an excellent example of each type would suffice, and a rug with very bad spots would not interest me at any price.

We do not find very many of the Persian, Turkish, Caucasian, or Turkoman rugs with bad spots. Many of the old plainer-field Chinese develop large spots that render them worthless.

The time when the aniline dyes ran into the other colors is no longer an issue. I don't recall seeing a single old, used rug of the old aniline dye period, which the old books of 60 years ago warned against, in the last five years. You are no longer concerned with the aniline dyes of the 1890–1917 period. These rugs are just not around. They have been worn out and discarded with rare exceptions.

One of the well-known types of rug will come with some slight bleeding and still be accepted by the expert. Some few of the finest quality old Bokharas, i. e., the Tekke (or Royal Bokhara), the Prayer Tekke (or Princess Bokhara), or the Salor Bokhara will have a little bleeding in the ivory. This is especially true of old tent bags. The exceptional wool quality, the vibrant wool with natural patina like tan velvet, and the exceptionally fine weave, will identify these particular rugs as being among the choicest and best specimens ever woven—except for this one fault. I can remember the little surprise I had when some of my teachers, who happened to be among the foremost experts of all time, told me this. Yes, you would like the same rug without this slight stain but you would buy it and not sell it until you found one of equal quality without this slight stain.

The above discussion was about the natural-colored rug—used, semi-antique, and the antique.

Somehow I don't think of the chemically washed and painted rug as bleeding or having loose colors, because they generally have the slight-to-bad stains where one color has overlapped the adjacent color, such as red design being on the edge of white, and the red color from the red design being on the adjacent blue design. Any one who has bought or will buy a used chemically washed and painted rug is not going to worry about this. But again, an old washed and painted Sarouk with fine, clean lines along the edge of the design instead of the usually muddy look is, in my judgment, still worth more. The medium-to-coarse quality Persians that have been both chemically washed and painted will almost invariably have a muddy or indistinct look, caused by a smear along the edge of the designs.

11. DRY ROT OR SALTWATER DAMAGE

The two are very akin to each other in that the area of the rug affected will be tender and easily broken. There is no way to correct either of these in most cases.

The dry rot is the result of the rug having laid on a damp floor for a long time, and then perhaps being in a home for many years. I can not tell you the specific reasons that cause some rugs to have this, but mainly it is being allowed to remain damp for a substantial period of time.

Many times a rug with such a tender spot has remained in a home on a pad without breaking. If it was in a heavy traffic lane, however, you can be sure it would break and come apart in that area.

How can you tell? It is most difficult to be sure on a large carpet size. On a small rug, you can take the rug in hand on the back and with each hand about a foot apart you apply pressure in a tug-of-war manner, and if it is tender you will hear it crack and you let up to keep from tearing a great slit. Trying other areas you can easily hear and feel it if it is tender in an area.

A large rug with a number of tender spots like this can lose 90% of its value on discovery. We would buy no rug with dry rot because there is no way to correct it.

If the damage is at one end of the rug, the best solution is to cut that end of the rug off and sew the border back on. If the border has tender areas of dry rot or you need the full size of the rug, there is one good solution and that is to glue on a piece of canvas cloth or rubber with glue or Lastex or similar material right to the rug, with the hope that this will prevent the breaks and tears. There is a good chance that the rug will go along for a good many years, but it loses its value.

Saltwater damage has the same effect as dry rot, or a worse effect. One might think that the rotten places from saltwater damage would be apparent right at the time the rugs arrived in this country and at the time they were inspected by Customs or the dealer. The bad and

Plate 23. KEEN-LING Chinese rug from India, saltwater damaged while en route. Insurance inspector found it easy to tear off the damaged areas. Salt water will completely rot a rug and there is no possible way to repair a rug damaged in this way except to remove the border.

worst damage will be discovered and the insurance company will pay the dealer and then turn around and have these sold either at auction or to some small jobbers in the market. I have watched two or three such dealers for many years and they do wonders in cutting and sewing when they buy the rug for little or nothing.

But where they misjudge is when an area of a rug which they thought was undamaged did, in fact, get a little salt water on it, although not enough to cause the damage to be apparent at the time. Over the years these spots or areas rot and they fall out.

THIS IS AN IMPORTANT CHECK BUT DON'T GET THE IDEA THAT VERY MANY RUGS WILL HAVE EITHER OF THESE FAULTS.

The only rug with a bad dry-rot condition that has any value would be a choice or rare small prayer rug or one suitable as a hanging. This would need backing with a cloth (not with glue) and would be alright if bought at a fraction of its perfect condition price.

121

12. JUFTI KNOTS

This item might have been omitted as only some of the rugs made since 1945 will have this fault. You will not readily detect this coarsening down of the weave. This is simply tieing the hand-tied knot on four warp strings instead of two. If the entire rug was woven in this manner you would have a rug with exactly half as many knots as the honest rug of the same type, and you would have a rug with half the amount of wool in the nap, and half as compact as it should be.

No rug, except some of the rugs from the Kurasan District, is woven entirely with the jufti knot, and this was typical of their weave for generations.

The jufti knot will be intermixed with the regular knot in many different types of rugs. The reason, of course, is so that the weaver can complete the rug in less time. Often the purpose is to be able to sell the rug at the same old price when the cost has gone up.

Many of our fine rugs, like the Nain, the best grade Kirmans, and others, will not have any of these false knots.

Finally, don't worry about this. The test for you to make is to check if one rug of the type is more compact than another of the same type. Even if your rug has many jufti knots, if it has a good nap of excellent wool quality, it is going to last a full lifetime. You must remember that many of the old, coarse tribal or nomad rugs wore a very long time; oftentimes longer than the more finely woven rug.

Of course, the more tightly woven a rug of the type, the better the rug, assuming that it has a good wool quality.

13. WHITE KNOTS IN RUG

White knots are present in many new oriental rugs when they are first woven. This is especially true of the Kirmans today, even the best Kirmans. These are removed or colored, but as the rug wears thinner with use they reappear.

These white knots are the end of the cotton warp strings on which the rug is woven. When the weaver sets up the cotton warp strings on his loom, there are many breaks in these cotton strings as he pulls them taut, or when he comes to the end of a ball of warp thread. There are thousands of these warp threads in a 9×12 ft. rug, and there are many of these tied together. When the rug is finished these often lie even with the wool nap, and are oftentimes longer. If the weaver has depressed these, when the rug is water washed in Iran, or chemically washed in New York, of even when it goes through the dusters or beaters before it is brought to the importer's showroom, they become visible.

There are two ways of handling these so they will not show in a new rug. One is to clip these white cotton threads a little shorter than the height of the nap. Usually they are snipped off with a pair of tweezers, or curved scissors. The other method is to touch them with a drop of dye or ink in the same color as the nap around the knots. The clipping with scissors is the preferred way.

As the rug wears down with years of use, the nap gets down to the same height of the cotton warp string. Then it must again be clipped.

If the rug is a chemically washed and painted rug, these white knots seem to appear in greater numbers. Of course, these were originally painted the same as the woolen nap, but in soap and water washing this dye comes off of these white cotton knots quite readily.

I have had many people come to me with their rugs which had been cleaned by a rug-cleaning plant, to ask what had happened when these knots appeared. They were sure that the cleaner had done something to their rug and had ruined it when it was returned with all the white knots showing. It was no fault of the cleaner, but he should have had sense enough to take a few minutes and retouch these (without charge). A matter of a few minutes on a small rug would save a real complaint. On a large rug where it would involve $15.00 to $25.00 in time to touch the hundreds of white knots that would appear if the rug was worn thin, he had better know how to explain this.

This is the kind of touching up that we approve of. The owner will say that these white knots were not there when they sent the rug to be cleaned, or that the cleaner ruined the rug as it was not so worn when sent in. Actually, when these white knots are badly soiled they are not too noticeable. They show up much more when the rug is cleaned, and of course in washing the dye will come off the cotton that has been touched. The wool will hold the dye better.

So, when you buy an old thin rug and it looks pretty good, you can be sure that when the worn areas are cleaned it is going to look much more worn. This is especially true of an old, thin, chemically washed and painted rug.

There is no way to repair or improve this condition except by touching up the worn areas. A very small area or several small areas can be re-woven or warp covered with flat tapestry-like stitch, but where there are sizable areas of worn-out spots, there is little than you can do, except paint in the background. This is a temporary measure and only a make-shift until you can afford another rug.

14. SPOTS ON RUG

This is a broad subject. It should not be a too difficult point for the buyer because they will know whether the spot is objectionable to them. Most large spots are objectionable and take away from the value of the rug. The tiny spots such as small burns the size of a pea to a dime in figured rugs, can readily be re-woven if they are not too numerous. Most antiques and semi-antiques that formerly came from Iran had a few of these.

THE MAIN POINT IS TO KNOW THE COST OF RE-WEAVING THESE IF THEY ARE OBJECTIONABLE TO YOU.

You will find a few small ink spots on almost every rug that has seen some use in the Orient. Again, these can be easily pulled out and re-woven if they are not too large.

The main spots to watch out for on a rug used in America are the badly discolored dog stains (from urine). If much of this is on the rug, the area becomes quite stiff and it can seldom be removed even with a thorough soap and water washing.

Although our canine friends are not going to damage 1 in 1,000 rugs in this manner, we do see a few valuable rugs each year that are thus completely ruined as far as resale value. This has not been the result of one accident or a half dozen accidents, but a repetition over a year or several years.

15. GLUE, LASTEX, OR NON-SKID SUBSTANCE ON BACK OF RUG

Recently a party from out of town shipped us a number of oriental rugs each of which had painted on the underside (back against floor), a so-called non-skid liquid. This was done to prevent the rug from slipping. It was heartbreaking to find these rugs made stiff and almost boardlike with the glue or Lastex on the underside. The rug that we might have paid $100.00 for was not worth more than $20.00 to $25.00. No one is going to buy these rugs unless they are very cheap, and then only as makeshift floor covering.

With this stiffening on the back, it was impossible to pass a needle through the rug for overcasting the sides or fixing the ends. Nor could small holes be fixed because you simply could not get the needle through this stiffness.

Who could have advised her to do this? I can understand why some inexpensive domestic rug that will have no resale value might be so treated.

There are materials to lay under a rug that will hold it in place and keep it from slipping or skidding, and thus eliminate the danger of a fall. We have used the thin non-skid by DUPONT for 46 years and it is most satisfactory. There are many excellent thick sponge-rubber rug paddings that act as both pad and non-skid. The thin DuPont non-skid and other similar material are probably more effective for small rugs and often for runners. These materials are simply laid on the floor and the rug placed on top.

16. CHINESE RUGS

A separate discussion of Chinese rugs is in order, even though one of the main points to check on in buying a used Chinese rug are the white knots. (Ends of tied warp threads showing on surface of nap.)

These white knots are more damaging in a Chinese rug than in any other type of rug. The reason for this being that the Chinese rugs of the period 1922 to 1934 had much open field without design, and it is difficult to touch these in many of the colors that the rugs come in. And it is a fact that the Chinese of that period had more of these white knots than any other rug I have ever seen. Also, the warp threads being larger in diameter than in the Persians, the white knots are much larger when the nap is worn thin.

I recall the period 1923–1934 when every importing house in New York that sold Chinese rugs had at least two or three people sitting at a long table and clipping or removing these knots. There would be at least a quart on a 9×12 ft. rug of these tiny cotton tips that were clipped to a lower height than the nap so that they would not be visible. This was done after the rug had been given a light chemical wash to give it the luster or silkiness. All imported Chinese rugs were given this light wash—at least 99 out of 100 were. No Chinese rugs were given the heavier chemical washing and painting process.

Many Chinese rugs that were not even lightly treated found their way into the country. Most of these were brought in by Army and Navy people who served in China. A rug called "Fette Rug" was popular with these service people. These rugs usually had more design and were entirely different from the some 90,000 Chinese rugs in 9×12 ft. size being woven in China each year by some 600 factories for export to America.

While these Fette rugs were not as heavy as the Nicols (one of the very best made) or most of the others, our table of experience tells us that these Fette rugs never seem to have these white knots and also they seem, as a whole, to be in better condition after 40 years use than the great mass of Chinese rugs appearing on the market from estates and resale.

The typical Chinese rug of that day is shown in my large book *Oriental Rugs—A Complete Guide,* in plate 191, and many came in the almost plain field like plate 187 (plate of Imperial), and later many came in the French Savonnerie designs on the order of plate 185.

Perhaps the Fette rugs did not have the white knots because Mrs. Fette, being an American who had set up her plant in China, would insist on each warp thread being a complete continuous string, and when the string broke or the ball came to an end, she would not tie this thread in the middle of the rug but rather would put in a continuous warp thread. This is a surmise on my part, but it almost certainly had to be the reason why we seldom find white knots in this type of Chinese rug.

The Sino-Japanese War around 1934 put an end to all rug weaving in China until recently. We do not trade with China and hence no new Chinese rugs come from there.

Again, the white knots generally mean that the rug is pretty well worn down, but some few poorer qualities will have a great deal of cotton mixed with the wool. Fortunately, most of these are worn out and seldom seen for sale.

Stains or Discoloration on Chinese Rugs

Bad stains on a Chinese rug detract greatly from its value. If the rug has much open plain field and the stains have not come out in a good soap and water washing, there is little you can do to make the rug salable. No matter how thick and otherwise good, a rug with big or easily noticeable stains becomes nearly worthless. You may be willing to pay $500.00 for the rug, but you wouldn't have it as a gift to use in your living room or dining room if the spot is an eyesore. Oftentimes, the nap on one of these Chinese rugs for some reason runs in a different direction from the rest of the rug. Instead of running from one end to the other, the nap for example runs crosswise. This cannot always be corrected if the traffic load for many years has brought this about.

IT IS BEST NOT TO BUY A USED CHINESE RUG UNLESS

Plate 24. FETTE CHINESE RUG, so-called by the Americans who owned the factory. Not made since 1934. Most of these are still in very good condition, and seldom do they have any white knots.

IT IS ALREADY CLEAN OR WITH THE AGREEMENT THAT YOU WILL BUY IT IF THE SPOTS COME OUT IN THE CLEANING.

We discuss prices under Point no. 19, but we will cover prices on Chinese rugs here.

Of all the used rugs that have been overpriced, I think a great many of the Chinese have to be counted in. If you are buying a rare, old Chinese and it is in fair condition (there are not many good ones), the rug is worth what you are willing to pay. Guide lines are not available to the extent they are in other types of oriental rugs.

But if you are buying one of those heavy qualities that were made in the period 1922–34, they should not be priced as objects of art, because after all they are simply floor covering. Back in the above period seldom did a Chinese rug cost the dealer over $2.25 per sq. ft. or, $245.00 for the rug (9 × 12). These retailed mostly for under $400.00 and seldom for more than $450.00. When someone tells you they paid, or their parents paid, $800.00 for a Chinese rug in 1928 or thereabouts, you can be sure that they were taken in because a handsome profit would have been made if the price were $495.00.

Now, that was 40 years ago, and many other types of orientals have doubled and trebled in value during that time even when sold as used rugs. Everything else has gone up, and with no Chinese rugs being imported since China became a Communist country, why wouldn't they be worth much more? Perhaps on the basis of supply and demand this could be true. Somehow, I have always reasoned that most Chinese rugs went down a little in value each year they were used. THIS IS JUST ONE MAN'S THINKING. I have seen some crazy prices on Chinese rugs in these used rug sales in New York. Rugs that I would want to sell for $100.00 to $150.00 sell for $500.00 or more. A real good one in 9 × 12 ft. size is worth $500.00 and perhaps more.

I say that I was never over enthusiastic about the Chinese rugs from China.

ACTUALLY, I LIKE MANY OF THE NEW RUGS BEING WOVEN IN INDIA IN MANY OLD CHINESE DESIGNS better than I like the old Chinese rugs. Perhaps this is because these new rugs from India are in the old Chinese designs and are more like the Fette rugs and some of those that our Army officers brought back from China. Also they come mainly in light decorative colors.

17. USED RUGS FROM INDIA

We are referring to the later day oriental rugs from India—those made since World War II.

Before the war, most of the rugs imported from India were very much like the Persian rugs. There were many of these such as Indo-Sarouk, Indo-Kirman, Indo-Feraghan, Indo-Ispahan, and many others in the early thirties such as the Laristan, and Kandahar, all in Persian design. Many of these were as lovely and as finely woven as the better Kashan of that day, and even much better than the Kirman of that period. The present-day contract-quality 80–40 Kirman are better than 99 percent of the Kirmans made during that period, 1915–1945. But you will see comparatively few of these Persian-type rugs from India and when you do you should consider them by the same yardstick as you would a Persian rug. NONE OF THESE WERE EVER CHEMICALLY WASHED AND PAINTED, though most of them had a very light lime wash or so-called plain washing to give the rug a little finish.

This discussion is to give information on the many thousands of rugs from India that are imported each year. Most of these are in the

Savonnerie designs and in the old Chinese designs. Others come in two tones and some few in Spanish design. The most popular seem to be those without too much design—those in the Savonnerie designs with much open plain field—on the order of the Kirmans.

We prefer the simple designs in preference to the ornate designs, but that is a matter of personal taste.

As already stated, these rugs are very popular in America and perhaps especially so because of their light pastel colors. We have told you that you need not be too much concerned with imperfections in these, though a few will come slightly wider at one end—not more than a couple of inches on a 9×12 ft.—and this is no real defect. And in buying one of these that has been used in America, you will need to be concerned only with its condition and the price. We have sold many thousands of these during the past 25 years, and they have proven themselves beyond question.

In buying a used one you do not have to worry about the white knots that show up in old Chinese rugs and which destroy the value of the rug. I attribute this to the fact that these British-trained Indians do not tie the warp threads together when one breaks in the middle of the rug, but rather they run a complete thread from the upper horizontal bar of the loom to the lower bar. I have not observed a single one of these rugs with white knots, and it is safe to say that I have sold more of these than any other dealer in the country. Even the lesser qualities do not have the white knots.

You should be concerned with the thickness, the tightness of weave, and especially any bad sizable spots. A large, bad spot can ruin the value of any rug, for who would want to live with an eyesore in a rug?

You will also want to check to see that it has not been overscrubbed with a heavy brush that might open out the ends of the nap and give it a woolly appearance.

BUT MAINLY YOU SHOULD BE CONCERNED WITH THE PRICE.

These lovely rugs, once they are used for a year or more, will not sell for as much as a new rug of the same size, type, and quality. We have been very explicit with our wonderful clientele and told them that if they moved and wanted to trade these in, they would have to take a substantial loss—assuming they were trading and not spending considerable more money in exchange.

You may ask why these are not as good an investment as the more colorful new Persians. The answer is simple. The colorful new Persian, when used, mellows and becomes more like a semi-antique or antique, and, in fact, in time does become a semi-antique or antique. Since these semi-old and old Persians are seldom available by importation any more, when one of these is traded, if the colors have mellowed, and if bought in the last 30 years the chances are that the nap is in very good condition. It may need renovation on sides and ends.

And if your rug was a semi-antique or antique when purchased, it probably has increased in value by reason of scarcity—the old law of supply and demand. Even when slightly thin these antiques will often bring more than you paid—provided you bought it at the right price.

A small country like Iran, with only a few million people, is producing fewer and fewer rugs each year, and with the industrialization taking place there, salaries are becoming higher each year. And it looks as though we will not have Iranian rugs in numbers for many more years.

So, why aren't the rugs from India more valuable as well? First, these rugs are made in soft pastel colors with chrome dyes. They are pale colors when first bought. If you are a prospective buyer and come into our store, and we show you a used Savonnerie from India or a Chinese from India, you will think it beautiful and probably would be willing to buy it. But when we show you the same rug completely new which has never been used and with the same soft colors as the used one, YOU ARE NOT GOING TO BE WILLING TO PAY THE SAME PRICE FOR THE USED ONE AS FOR THE NEW ONE. To be sure, the used one may be slightly softer, but the new one is already soft and exquisite.

And you must take it from me that 99 out of 100 buyers will buy the new rug in the same colors and same design, if the new one is only $50.00 higher than the used one.

I do not wish for one moment to disparage these lovely rugs. They may not be the investment that the Persians often prove to be, but they are wonderful when compared to the broadloom. Wonderful as to durability and to beauty and, of course, they always have some value.

There are some 400,000,000 people in India and raising the standard of living there for this great number is going to be ten times harder than doing this in Iran with a smaller population. I might add that the United States has spent perhaps a billion dollars in aid to Iran. Our chapter on "Outlook for the Future on Oriental Rugs," goes into further detail. India is the main hope for hand-made oriental rugs in the future. Already, some 2,000,000 people are engaged in the rug-weaving industry there.

130

The fact that you may take a loss on the cost price in trading an Indian rug for a different size rug should not be discouraging, because they are far less expensive per years' use than any wall to wall carpeting. Most of these will outlast two or three sets of broadloom.

18. IS THE RUG A REAL HANDMADE ORIENTAL OR A MACHINE-MADE COPY?

We have covered this subject under "Discussion in Buying New Orientals." A used MACHINE-MADE COPY of an oriental rug has very little resale value. We have never once taken a one in trade nor ever offered to sell one.

It is surprising how many estates will have one or more of these mixed with their oriental rugs. Usually, the heirs of the party offering them will have a suspicion that they are not the real oriental rugs even though they have never before owned an oriental rug.

Anyone who has lived with oriental rugs will almost invariably know at a glance that the rug is not a real oriental.

If the copy is so good (and I don't know of such a copy) and you have no expert advice nearby, I suggest that you open out the nap and examine the base of the nap. If it is a real oriental rug you will see the knots (loops tied) at the base of each two strands of nap. If it is machine made there will be no knot. The strands of thread will have been attached to the base by a machine.

Of course, if you ever buy such a rug thinking it to be a real oriental and later find that you have bought the machine-made rug, you should report it to the BETTER BUSINESS BUREAU of your CHAMBER OF COMMERCE.

19. PRICES

The price of used rugs is perhaps the most difficult subject one could choose to discuss.

In the first place any prices we gave you today will, no doubt, be out of date in another five or ten years. Even since I started writing this book, great changes have occurred in Iran that have or will increase prices on Iranian rugs.

We hope that in the general discussions of the many points covered, you have gained some information that will be helpful as to prices.

Probably the best current information we can hope to furnish will be for you to request one of our descriptive lists at the time. This will give you prices on many different types. It will not be complete information, but it will be the same general information we would give you if you wrote in to us.

When we speak of prices of used rugs, you must remember that the used rug could be antique, semi-antique, or a worn rug. There are many used rugs which we do not wish to compliment with the title semi-antique or antique. If it happens to be a used chemically treated rug, it will always be in the USED RUG category, and never will be classed as antique or semi-antique, no matter how old it is.

THE MAIN POINTS TO CONSIDER UNDER PRICE OF ANY RUG ARE CONDITION AND RARITY. Rarity covers a broad field as the rug could be merely a utility rug or an art piece suitable for a collection.

Always we have to remember that rugs by the same name vary greatly as to weave, wool quality, and beauty. So, two rugs of the same name and same general condition could vary greatly as to value.

We have told you that a used rug in good condition is usually worth more than a new rug of the same type. The exceptions to this are the Persian rugs that have been chemically washed and painted, and the Chinese rugs, and also, as a rule, the rugs from India.

How can I give you a rule of thumb for any one type—because an unscrupulous dealer could fail to give you the line of demarcation between rugs of the same name.

Take the name Kirman, which is one of the highest priced and best of new rugs being woven today. The oldest, finest, and rarest of these is the Laver Kirman. These were woven in the old town of Ravar, some 50 miles from today's great rug-weaving center by that name. These were exceptionally fine-woven, thin rugs and have a high value even if worn thin. Of course, very little if threadbare, except for a museum (and I still like those in a museum to have some little nap left). Most of these came in the so-called Dozar size, a rug about $4\frac{1}{2} \times 6\frac{1}{2}$ ft. Many people bought these as Kirmanshah (also spelled Kermanshah). The name Kirmanshah would not interest the collector; the Laver Kirman is much more valuable.

Around the turn of the century rugs were woven in and around Kirman in somewhat similar designs to those in Lavers. The principal features were a creamy ivory field with an intricate floral centerpiece (medallion) and corners, and finely drawn vines over the field. These so-called Kirmanshahs were usually given a light chemical bath to soften the colors, but they were never painted like so many of the other Persian rugs were. Some few came in small sizes, but most were in dozar sizes and carpet sizes (9 × 12 ft. and larger).

The Kirmanshah was never a correct name for these rugs because they were woven in and around Kirman, while the Town of Kirmanshah was 1,000 miles to the west, a Kurdish mountain town not too far from the Turkish border. Any rugs by the Kurds would have been much coarser and entirely different, but the name has been used so much by dealers that there is no harm, and is generally accepted, though not by any collector or expert.

Also, from about 1875 to about 1910, most of the Kirmans in scatter sizes came with entirely different designs than Kirmans of the past 60 years. Many used an allover design such as small baskets of flowers or vases with flowers. And many of these did not have the ivory background.

Then came the big rush period of 1920–1932. Most of the Kirmans switched their designs to the same general design as the Sarouks were using with the blue field, or red field, and with an allover detached floral design. Why they changed is not understandable, unless, as we remember, the Sarouks at that time cost about $1.00 to $2.00 more per sq. ft. (wholesale) than the Kirmans did. These Kirmans were almost invariably chemically washed and painted like the Sarouks. It was the only period that Kirmans were so treated. I recall the first time I went abroad I was glad to buy a few Kirmans that had only the light 2% lime wash.

These went out with the depression and most of them wore out as well. The wool quality was usually not as good as that in Sarouks. So, when one of these appears from an estate, it is usually badly worn after 40 years and is worth only $50.00 to $250.00 in the 9 × 12 ft. size. Of course, one in good condition would be worth more.

The period 1932–1941 continued with some few of the above rugs, but most were woven in the light background and with more design than most of the present-day Kirmans with much open plain field.

During this period the Kirman most preferred by Persians and Europeans was the densely covered design—the field would be covered with vine, leaf, and floral designs. This was the so-called classical period referred to by A. Cecil Edwards.

Next we have the Kirman of the last 25 years. And the best quality of these is one of the best rugs woven today (one of the 3 or 4 best rugs woven in Iran). These top quality Kirmans, which we call 80–40 quality, contract-quality, and which are lightly bleached, will wear a full lifetime and perhaps two lifetimes and be valuable property. A used one of these will not sell for quite as much as the same quality new Kirman, but it will bring a big price.

Quickly, I must remind you that the above applies only to the contract-quality, that is, specially made by contract for American dealers. For these the finest grade of wool is brought in instead of using the local wool.

Another quality of Kirman being woven today is known as the Bazaar quality. This is a quality woven in the homes by individuals or families. The local Iranian market and the European market use most of these. It is, as a rule, not nearly so heavy as the 80–40 contract-quality, nor does it, as a rule, have the excellent wool quality, and most of them are not nearly as finely woven. However, some of these Bazaar qualities can be very finely woven and still wear down very quickly because of the poor wool used.

Some time ago, an Iranian graduate student at Syracuse University, whose home town was Kirman, brought in his 9×12 ft. Kirman to show me and ask why it had worn so thin in about 5 to 7 years in his home here in America. I explained to him that it was due to the wool quality of his Bazaar quality Kirman. Probably in his home in Kirman they took off their shoes as they entered the house, and I forget if I asked him if he had fallen for American gadgets such as the electric cleaner.

NOW ALL OF THE ABOVE REFERS TO ONE NAME. How could I possibly go about giving you specific information as to what you should pay for a $4\frac{1}{2} \times 6\frac{1}{2}$ ft. Kirman, or one 9×12 ft.

True, not all the names will be quite as confusing, and if they are you can see where we could write 500 pages on prices alone.

ONE MORE TYPE DESERVES SOME LITTLE DISCUSSION. For some 100 years the name Sarouk has been well known. To many of us in the trade it meant a chemically washed and painted rug until some 14 years ago. Some few still are being painted and we have covered that under that heading.

The early Sarouks, from about 1800 to 1910, were among the choicest of Persian rugs. They are woven in the village of Sarouk which lies in the Feraghan Plains. One of the best Sarouks was as choice and as rare as the best Feraghan. Even the thin ones that are not completely worn out are very valuable today.

Around 1900 they began to lightly bleach these and so, when one of these finely woven thin examples appears, it has a somewhat faded appearance. These will not interest the experts but they bring good prices because of their light faded colors.

Also, around this time, when the demand in America became so great and when practically all the Sarouks had been made with the medallion design, an allover design was created to please American decorators. This design has been the main design for most Sarouks made for the American trade during the past 50 years—up to a few years ago.

AND AS WE EXPLAINED IN GREAT DETAIL UNDER THE CHEMICALLY WASHED AND PAINTED section, both under check points for new rugs and check points for used rugs, 95 per cent of these were chemically bleached and painted. These Sarouks, even with this treatment, have given a good account of themselves as far as durability is concerned.

BUT THEY DO NOT HAVE THE RESALE OR TRADE-IN VALUE THAT THE UNTREATED RUGS DO, WHETHER ANTIQUE OR NEARLY NEW.

I should have told you about the very excellent Josan Sarouks that are very superior little rugs, and which almost invariably increase in value. Use only improves them—that is, until they get real old and show some wear. This doesn't seem to happen during the first 50 years' use.

The Malayer Sarouk was a Sarouk made in a city some distance from Sarouk. As a rule, it was not as fine and not as heavy, but always in the old traditional designs.

We have told you that for some years there has been very little chemical washing and painting of oriental rugs. A small percentage of the Sarouks still are so processed. But the cost of labor in the two Long Island plants made dealers seek to have these softened with a light treatment in Iran, or only the light chemical bath in these American plants. The light wash in Iran does very little to tone the color and it is little more, if anything more, than a water wash. For a very good reason, the light chemical washing of Sarouks has nearly stopped. I am sure that this is mainly because the dyes in the Sarouks are different combinations of colors to produce one color, and too many bad hairbrushes or changes of color appear when the rug is chemically bleached and then the rug of necessity has to be painted—a costly process today.

Now, the good news about Sarouks. A good number of this weave or name are coming in or being woven in two lovely antique designs, as opposed to the typical Sarouk with red field and allover detached floral design (the one we said had to be washed and painted to be very salable).

The new SARABEND SAROUK is one of the best rugs being woven in Iran today. It is my opinion that it is as durable as any rug to be had today. Here the Sarouk simply uses the small allover Sarabend design —a small, repetitive floriated pear design—and they take the Sarabend border design. The field (background) may be red, rosy red, navy, ivory, or gold. You will not find a used one of these over 10 years old, but a few years' use will have softened the colors even nicer than when new.

The latest change in the Sarouk situation is the appearance of a good number of these in the ivory or cream background with an allover design taken from some of the old Ispahans of 300 to 400 years ago. My color Plate No. 98 in my large book gives a typical one of these. They are learning to use some rather soft blues, greens, gold, and rose instead of too much red.

Again, one of these with a few years' use should sell for as much or more than the completely new rug. This is not necessarily so because many of these are being made in very delightful shades.

For the development of the Sarabend Sarouk and the classical 16th century or Ispahan design Sarouk, we are indebted to the Germans. They did not like our typical Sarouk—the red field with the allover detached floral designs.

SO, ONCE AGAIN, HOW CAN I INFORM YOU AS TO THE PRICE YOU SHOULD PAY FOR A USED SAROUK?

We could make an equally long or longer discussion of the different types and qualities of Herez and Gorevans. And the same would be true of Tabriz rugs. We could do the same about Kashans, as well as the many types from the Meshed District, where the quality will vary from the superior Turkbaff (what most dealers call Ispahan) to the junkiest type of Khorasan. (Birjands).

BUT, MAINLY, OUR DETAILED DISCUSSION SHOULD HELP YOU BE ALERT. WHEN BUYING AN EXPENSIVE RUG, IF YOU DO NOT KNOW RUGS, PERHAPS YOU SHOULD SEEK THE ADVICE OF SOME FRIEND WHO HAS A LITTLE KNOWLEDGE.

This may be dangerous advice, because I have seen a few people willing to give very opinionated advice when they had no knowledge on the subject.

ONE MORE POINT ON WHICH I WILL WARN YOU. Don't be influenced too much by what the people tell you they have paid for the rug, or what their parents paid for the rug. And, I might add, or what some dealer had told them the rug was worth when they were charged $200.00 to repair the rug. I hate to mention that point, but some few dealers really have been way off base, or shall we say, plain dishonest. When a fine couple told me they had paid $750.00 a year previously for a certain rug for which I offered them $150.00 in trade (not $150.00 cash), I suggested that they go back to the dealer and offer to take a different rug in trade that would be priced $350.00, and take a loss of $400.00. The little dealer wouldn't take it back at any price. There are not many crooks like this in permanent rug stores today.

You must not be over influenced by what the owners (whether the owners or the heirs) say the rug originally cost. These people are honest in 99 out of 100 cases. Their parents got these ideas of value probably from an appraiser (and not one in a hundred is qualified to appraise oriental rugs—I have been asked for help by a hundred of them), or some repairman who sought the repair job and overvalued the rug, or some friends telling them they are worth so much.

Actually, the original owners themselves often think they have paid twice as much as they really paid. When we go to our files and present the copy of the sales slip, showing date, size, name and price, they are flabbergasted. I have never known a single case of this kind where my good friends had the least intention of being dishonest. I always shake their hand and say, "What I like about these rugs is the fact that you value them so dearly."

Oftentimes, WE HAVE BEEN WILLING TO ALLOW THEM TWICE WHAT THEY PAID FOR THE RUG 25 to 40 YEARS AGO. Recently, I paid $275.00 for a 4 × 6 ft. rug which I sold in 1930 for $75.00. We would have given $400.00 in trade. The rug now hangs in my office as it was the first rug I ever owned.

Many people did pay some very fancy prices during the boom years 1920–1930, when there were no income taxes. In my large book, *Oriental Rugs—A Complete Guide,* I recite the case where the president of one of the big auto manufacturing companies paid $5,000.00 each for five 9 × 12 ft. Kashans, or a total of $25,000.00. These rugs wholesaled at that time for $10.00 per sq. ft., or $1,080.00 for each 9 × 12 ft. rug. A right selling price might have been $1,625.00, or even $1,900.00, which would be the gross profit required by many dealers. I was present in this great store in 1924 when this happened and often discussed the transaction with the manager of this department. Of course, they had priced some of the same rugs that cost the same $1,080.00, for less than $1,500.00 on sale. They had bought a group of Kashans and graded them according to their judgment as to beauty and value.

It was the same case where a $1,000.00 ring is not good enough for the very wealthy and a slightly better ring worth little more is selected for $3,000.00.

This is still being done by many dealers but perhaps not to this extent. And it is right to grade rugs you buy in a group, because one is often worth twice what the other is of the same name and size. But the $5,000.00 price was out of line. Over the years I have seen many rugs bought at ridiculous prices.

When a person who knows nothing whatever about oriental rugs walks in a home where there is a private sale or estate sale, they have a pretty good chance of getting a good value. The conductor of the sale either has some information from the owners, or gets someone in to help who does know. And generally they have had considerable experience and know whether the rug is fine, worn, is the real thing, or a machine-made copy.

We definitely cannot teach you how to become expert or know rugs overnight, but we believe that if you read all we have written in this present book, you will avoid many of the pitfalls. YOU WILL AT LEAST BE ALERTED AS TO WHAT TO CHECK.

Our Chapter Twelve, on "Classifications and Resume," will be of still further assistance. We debated including this chapter.

Chapter Eight

CHANGES SINCE PUBLICATION OF MY LARGE BOOK

We need to note or call your attention to many important changes that have occurred since I wrote my large book, *Oriental Rugs—A Complete Guide,* some eight years ago (published by Charles E. Tuttle Co., Rutland, Vt. & Tokyo, Japan).

There has been a great improvement in quality in many of the types, and some deterioration in quality in others, but the balance of these lies on the plus or improvement side.

A number of factors have contributed to the improvement, and I think we have to give European countries, and especially Germany, the credit for bringing about much of the improvement in quality, designs, and colors. We have to remember that it is only since World War II that Europeans in great numbers have had the wealth to buy the better rugs. For many years I visited the London market (the market for European buyers and dealers) during the period about 1928 until World War II, and it was my impression that except for the rugs confiscated by the Russians, the great mass of Persian rugs sent to the London market were mostly of the poorer qualities. Many thin fine rugs, such as new Ispahans and Kashans, were available there, but only because they were new and bright and stiff looking, and not heavy enough to withstand the chemical washing that American dealers wanted to give most of their rugs at that time.

For years I believed that the Europeans liked too many rugs—that they liked any rug so long as they could say it was oriental—and frankly stated that Americans had better taste as far as oriental rugs are concerned. The Europeans did insist on the traditional designs.

I still will not retract that statement 100 percent today. Last spring I was in London with two of my assistants and we saw many oriental rugs in the display window of a very large store. Each of us agreed that we would have a very hard time selling any of the rugs displayed at any price. They were truly horrible.

But let us not forget that these same European dealers have come to America and carted back to Europe two thirds of the rare antiques that have appeared at small dealers in New York. I do agree with them so wholeheartedly in that they want their rugs to be in traditional designs. Most Europeans do not want any newly created designs.

That brings us to the Sarouk rug. They have always disliked our typical allover detached floral design Sarouk (Plate 53 in our large book) that has been so popular in America for the past 60 years. So, it was only natural for them to order Sarouks in some of the best of the antique Sarouk designs and other types. The two best Sarouks, as a result of this, are the Sarabend Sarouks, and the Sarouk with an old Ispahan design very much like the color Plate No. 98 in our large book.

The Sarabend Sarouks take their design from the old Sarabends which were woven in a district about 30 miles from Arak. The field may be red, blue, ivory, or gold, and will have the tiny allover floriated pear design. Some few of these will have a small medallion and small corners. These Sarabend Sarouks, as a rule, are even better quality than our typical Sarouk.

Lately, a good many Sarouks have come in with the old 16th-century Ispahan design. Most of these have ivory field with an allover design consisting of old Shah Abbas motifs, tulips, vines, leaf, and floral design.

When I wrote my large book these two items were just beginning to appear. It is only lately that we are able to buy several of these Ispahan-Sarouks at one time.

The Kashan, one of the finest and best rugs woven, requires some comment. Most of these have come in some shade of red or blue—occasionally ivory—in the general design of Plate 40 in my large book. While the medallion in this rug was seldom conspicuous, and the design one of our favorites, I have to admit that the change in design in so many of these present-day Kashans is most pleasing. They are, in fact, almost identical in design to the Sarouk we discussed above—employing the old Ispahan design consisting of Shah Abbas motifs, finely drawn leaf, vine, and floral designs, and sometimes some of the old Chinese cloudbanks. These have a creamy ivory field, a light blue field, or a pale pastel green field. Most of these are in 9 × 12 ft. size, and approximately 10 × 14 size—a few larger. Unless the changes taking place in Iran send these much higher, they are sure to be one of the 3 or 4 most desirable of all Persian carpets.

Plate 25. NAIN from Iran. Among the finest rugs ever woven in Iran, including the past several hundreds of years. All are practically new, but they employ only the old 16th-century Ispahan design. In many of them the design is outlined in silk. Main part of the nap is wool. They contain six hundred knots to the square inch, which means that in this example, approximately 8×5 feet, there are some four million hand-tied knots! Incredible!

BUT THE BIG CHANGES OF THE PAST EIGHT YEARS IN IRAN (IMPROVEMENT INDUSTRIALLY) FAR OUTWEIGH THE CHANGES IN THE DIFFERENT TYPES OF RUGS.

The rapid industrialization of Iran over the past 8 years should be the biggest news to any dealer and those who like oriental rugs. More than ever before they can count their good oriental rugs as valuable property, and property likely to increase in value DOWN THROUGH THE YEARS.

THE UNITED STATES HAS SPENT OVER ONE BILLION DOLLARS IN AID TO IRAN SINCE WORLD WAR II. Certainly most of this has been spent to keep Iran out of the Russian sphere and in the American camp. The following are EXTRACTS FROM THE U.S. NEWS AND WORLD REPORT issue of January 27, 1969, under the title, "A MIDEAST 'VICTORY' FOR U.S.--THE BOOM IN IRAN."

141

"Brightest spot in shaky Middle East is the ancient kingdom of Iran. An economic revolution is lifting it out of the past, creating a modern nation that has set it sights high."

"Teheran, Iran: The biggest boom of modern times in the Middle East is suddenly transforming Iran into the most prosperous major country of the region—an oasis of stability in one of the world's most volatile areas."

"You see signs of the evolution the minute you enter this sprawling, traffic-choked city of nearly 3 million. Skyscrapers rise alongside bazaars, and miniskirted girls stroll with their mothers who wear the traditional 'chadors'—head-to-foot shawls."

"Economists say the boom, in size and scope, is unprecedented in the area."

THE NEXT BIG QUESTION MARK is the Iranian Shah's statement as to increase in rug weaver's wages and elimination of child weaving. Read beginning of Chapter Nine. Now, it is our observation and information that 75 percent of all the weavers in these industrialized towns like Teheran, and to a lesser extent Hamadan, were children under 12 years of age. The grown people have for some time been able to earn much more in the factories. This, of course, will not prevent children from weaving in the home in outlying and remote districts.

WE DISCUSS THESE TWO IMPORTANT CHANGES IN MORE DETAIL IN OUR CHAPTER NINE ON "OUTLOOK FOR THE FUTURE ON ORIENTAL RUGS."

HERE ARE SOME OF THE SPECIFIC CHANGES OF THE PAST 8 YEARS.

We have already discussed the favorable changes and development in Sarouk rugs.

PROBABLY THE GREATEST IMPROVEMENT IN QUALITIES HAS BEEN IN RUGS FROM THE HEREZ DISTRICT. There were many old and semi-old Herez rugs, as well as thousands of the best contract-quality (new) Herez, for the first several years after the war. Then, for a period of several years, the New York market was flooded with the coarsest and cheapest grade of Gorevans which were offered as Herez. Not only were they cheap in quality, but they used very poor dyes—a brownish dirty red; a dirty dead-looking blue —resulting in an altogether poor and unattractive rug. And worse still, many of these had used dead wool (butchered sheep wool).

We have not seen these in the past few years in the New York market or in the markets abroad. My conclusion is that the demand by the

Figure 8. Transition in Iran. Not too many years ago the only means of transportation was by donkey or camel. Now good roads, planes, factories, and great wealth from the oil fields is transforming Iran very rapidly.

Germans for Herez is so great that they contracted and demanded better quality. Yes, the Herez rugs are a favorite of the Germans, and some of those being woven today are as tight and as good as a Sarouk and nearly as costly.

HERE IS TRULY ONE OF THE GREAT IMPROVEMENTS. The NAIN rug, which is appearing in goodly numbers in the New York market, is certainly one of the brightest spots in rug weaving in Iran, or in the entire history of rug weaving. Very few of the fine rugs woven hundreds of years ago were as finely woven.

These are being woven in the town by that name which is very near Ispahan. Never in my 46 years in the oriental rug business has any other type as a class come so finely woven. Not even the real old Ispahans have the some 600 or more hand-tied knots to the square inch that these Nains have. Most of these are coming in sizes approximately 8 × 5 ft. with some 40 sq. ft. and over 4,000,000 knots to each rug. A small number are in the 3 × 5 ft. size, occasionally one 7 × 11 ft., and 2 or 3 large sizes are seen in the market each year. Not one rug in a hundred in all the museums of the world is so finely woven. The Ardabil Mosque Carpet in the Victoria & Albert Museum in London has only 340 knots to the square inch. This is the world's most famous and most valuable rug.

The fine silk Hunting Carpet in the Austrian Museum in Vienna does have some 780 knots to the inch.

143

There were a limited number of Nains available 10 years ago, but the availability today of these extremely finely woven rugs—actually finer than any other type that has been produced in Iran during the past 60 years—is almost unbelievable.

It is my guess that in years to come these rugs will be worth a King's ransom.

There is no great change in the Kirman situation with possible exception that most of the Kirmans coming to America are the excellent 80–40 quality, with only a few of the slightly lesser qualities.

The bad changes have come in the Hamadan District, but we also note some improvement recently in some few of the many types woven in that great rug-weaving district.

The deterioration in quality and workmanship of the inexpensive but well-liked Kapoutarhang was marked a few years ago, but in the past few months we have noted some improvement. The chief fault was a coarsening of the weave, too many jufti knots, and especially the poor, uneven clipping of the pile.

Two other rugs in the same general coloring of the Kapoutarhangs of 10 years ago (even nicer colors) are being made in much better rugs. They are the so-called Ramishan and the Gunjetepeh. The Ramishan is only slightly better than the Kapoutarhang while the Genjetepeh is an excellent quality rug. A good average weave, heavy nap, and very superior wool. Few other rugs made in Iran today, unless it be the Nain, have such rich, superior wool quality. The bright reds come very much like some Kirmans in design, and the ivory backgrounds whose designs are more colorful than the Kirman, will, in my opinion, last as long as any rug costing twice as much.

One of our very favorite of all rugs during the past 30 years has slipped greatly in quality, even though they have improved the colors. And that is the Kasvin. If anyone wanted a Kirman and could take a least bit more color in the design, they could go to this tightly woven heavy rug for less than the price of a Kirman. Most of those with the ivory background are so like the Kirman in design, though not as finely woven. Nor, do they have the light treatment that all Kirmans (or at least 99 percent of them) get after they get to America.

The main fault has been the uneven clipping. Rugs are hand-clipped and one must expect slight variations in the height of the nap, but for two or three years past we had to reject 4 out of 5 for this fault. We are glad to note that there seems to be an improvement on this during the past year.

144

Also, a new color has been brought out for the Kasvin. It is a light brilliant red, almost a rosy red, but whatever tint you give it, it is a most delightful, colorful rug, and so much more beautiful than the deep brownish or almost plum red fields with which most of these came when I wrote my large book eight years ago.

Another development has been the Mishkin rugs. This is a heavy type rug in geometric designs, woven in Northern Iran and copying the designs of the old Kazaks, Carabaughs, Kabistans, and other Caucasian rugs. Right after the war we were introduced to the Ardabil, a rather thin type rug on the order of the thinner Caucasian rugs, i.e., Kabistan, Shirvan, and Daghastans. We think these Mishkins are going to be better buys and more suitable for heavy traffic than the thinner Ardebils. The demand for the geometric rugs from Caucasia will make those who do not have to have antiques very happy. These should prove to be better investments in years to come because the Caucasian rugs are already overpriced due to the European buyers. As we have said, they have already carted off to Europe most of the choice, old Caucasian rugs from every dealer in America. Exception—for 10 years I have refused to sell these for export regardless of what they would offer me.

The small Hamadans, in 2×3 ft. and $2\frac{1}{2} \times 4$ ft. size that were so coarse and inexpensive (and yet good-looking, durable, and salable) have improved in one respect. Ten years ago there were thousands of these had been woven with poor blue dyes (that is, the part of the rug that was blue) and a blue weft was used. When these were washed in the river or even with a light lime wash in Iran, the blues discolored the white corners completely. If the nap seemed white on the surface, you only had to open it out and find the blue just beneath the nap surface. One could search through 100 of these small rugs and have difficulty finding a dozen without this dye. I wonder what became of many of these rugs. I believe I can tell you that many that have been cleaned (with soap and water) have lost much of this blue by rinsing, and in most that still have it, it does not show and does not bother the owners. Most people don't know this, and at $24.00 to $35.00 for one of these they are not hurt much, and especially since they don't notice it. The majority of these little inexpensive rugs of 8 to 15 years ago will show no wear whatsoever. Another rug (domestic rug) for which you paid the same amount is probably pretty sick looking today. The point is that even one of the less expensive of orientals is less expensive than any other type of floor covering—and better looking too.

Another finely woven Persian rug in the same general category as the

145

Kashan has come to America in numbers for the first time in 10 years. I refer to the Qum (also spelled Ghoum and Koum). They come mostly in Dozar sizes, especially $6\frac{1}{2} \times 4\frac{1}{2}$ ft. A limited number come about 7×10 or 7×11 and a few somewhat larger.

I repeat that rugs by the same name vary greatly in quality and value. Thus many of the different types that come are being woven in superior quality, while others of the same type have been cheapened down for price. But there is no great change in this condition.

So much for the changes in Iran and there WILL BE MANY MORE GREATER CHANGES IN THE NEXT FEW YEARS.

CAUCASIAN RUGS

The change we should note here on the small geometric Caucasian rugs such as Kazak, Kabistan, Daghestan, Shirvan, and the many others, is that the supply of these at dealers has diminished to nearly the zero point. The few that come from estates are quickly snapped up by European buyers and the prices have gone up out of all proportion.

You see some few new rugs in the London market from Caucasia that have been lightly treated, but these have not come to America. At the moment I would say that the Persian Mishkin is a better rug and a better buy, and it has the same general characteristics as a Caucasian.

TURKISH RUGS

No rugs have been woven in Turkey to any extent on a commercial basis for over 30 years. When the standard of living went up to $1.00 a day or more, weavers could not compete with the Iranian rugs at a few cents a day. A few rugs are being woven in Turkey as evidenced by service people (Army, Navy, etc.) and oil company employees bringing back some of these rugs. They are not imported in America for sale and they would not be successful to any great extent. We have refused to take in trade a number that people have wanted to exchange or sell. Turkish rugs are of no consequence to the layman today, except the old pieces from estates.

BOKHARA OR TURKOMAN RUGS

The big change here is the large production of hand-woven rugs in Western Pakistan in the old Bokhara design, principally in the Tekke or Royal design, and also a good number in the Salor design, in the last few years. All features of these rugs are geometric. They were available 8 years ago but the prices were much higher at that time. The Pakistani government, evidently in its desire for dollars, subsidized these so that good numbers are being woven. The LaHore quality, while not as heavy as the superior Karachi quality, costs no more than the lesser expensive and much coarser Iranian rugs. There are very few rugs better and more durable than the superior Karachi quality. All of this is based on your wanting the geometric design and not the floral.

One other change to note is that these Bokharas are, for the first time in history, being made with the ivory background, as well as gold, light blue, and a limited number of navy and green. The ivory is a particular favorite. However, two-thirds of them are still being made in the different shades of red and wine. At the present time these Bokharas are perhaps the greatest value on the market by reason of the subsidy.

RUGS FROM AFGHANISTAN

These come under the same heading as the Bokhara family. These deep wine red rugs, seldom with any light colors and with large geometric octagon design, have undergone two great changes. One is that these rugs are being made in better quality, tighter, heavier, and better wool than even the best old Afghans or Kiva Bokharas of 50 years ago.

The other change is the appearance of GOLD AFGHANS. These deep red Afghans are being given a special kind of treatment in London where the color is faded to a copperish gold. They are being brought to America in limited numbers and sold as Gold Afghans at fantastic prices. We offer no advice on buying these.

RUGS FROM INDIA

The big change in rugs from India has been the large number of small factories or operators offering rugs in hundreds of different designs and colors. Eight years ago there were only 3 or 4 importers dealing in rugs from India. Today there are dozens of importing houses offering rugs from India in many different qualities. And even though the Indian government de-valued their money, the price remains the same because they immediately raised wages from 17¢ to 28¢ a day—wages fixed by the government. No wonder we can get such beautiful hand-made rugs for so little money.

147

Another big change—eight years ago in the London market there were tens of thousands of poor grade rugs from India, too poor for the American trade. On our last few trips abroad few rugs from India were to be seen in London. The demand in America for these has provided a market for better rugs. Many very fine qualities are available.

RUGS FROM JAPAN

The industrial improvement in Japan has led to such sharp increases in prices that it has practically eliminated the importation of Japanese rugs which were in Chinese design. The excellent Imperial comes only in handfuls as it costs as much as a Kirman. My good friend who brings these in is finding that he can have a rug made in India for less than half. So far the quality has not been quite as good as the Imperial, but I predict that he will have that shortly. The last time I inquired about Imperials the wholesale price was somewhere around $8.00 to $10.00 a sq. ft. Few people are going to be willing to pay $1,500.00 for a 9×12 in this rug.

In our big book we praise the Fuji Royal. This completely disappeared from the market several years ago due to the increase in cost. The one importing house that brings in the Peking from Japan continues with a few of these. Their prices have not gone up as much as the others, but they are up sharply and these rugs will probably eliminate themselves if they have further increases.

CHINESE RUGS

In our big book, we said that no Chinese rugs had been made for 30 years. A limited number are now seen in the London market in excellent quality but the price is too high to be very salable in numbers in America. And we may import nothing from China.

There are some rugs being woven in Taiwan in Chinese design and in very good quality. So far only one importing house has brought them in and they are doing very well with them even though the price is likely to limit great volume. They are better than the Peking made in Japan which is a very good rug.

ONE DANGER—RUGS FROM HONG KONG

I do not know what is being woven in Hong Kong except some rugs that are being bought by people thinking they are real oriental. The rugs are hooked with a large, tight, wool yarn. If the back were not covered with the plastic you would notice the knots—very few to the inch. Some look to be as large as the end of your little finger. One concern in New York brings these in, and they are good-looking. They are not cheap as they should be with so little labor compared to the finer hand-woven rug. The daughter of a very wealthy person was charged $2,000.00 to have one custom made and was truly dumbfounded when she wished to trade it in to be told that it was a hooked rug. However, they are better than any hooked rug I have ever seen, but to my mind, overpriced. So, I will not mention the trade name of them. There may be some real oriental rugs woven in Hong Kong, but you do not have to have any real knowledge to look at the underside and discover if the rug is a real oriental or a hooked rug.

Chapter Nine

OUTLOOK FOR THE FUTURE
ON ORIENTAL RUGS

Our discussion in Chapter Eight should give you much information on what to expect in Iran. Since the vast majority of all carpet sizes are from Iran, and have been for the last 35 years, the outlook is indeed dark. It is dark for the dealer and the people who expect to accumulate rugs. For those who already own *good* rugs, they will find their property more valuable every year. The only chance of this not being completely correct is to have a recession in Europe and reduce their demand for Persian rugs. I am writing this book right at the very time of greatest agitation as to price—and the sharpest increase in prices. The Shah of Iran has announced on a number of occasions that the rug weavers' wages and standard of living had to be raised and that the children have to go to school. The dealers in Teheran, and in other big markets in Iran, believe he means business now. Immediately there has been a substantial increase in prices. But this is not too terrifying yet, when we realize that the daily wages for rug weavers is from 5 rials per day, to 35 rials per day for the master weavers who work on Kirmans. This means 15¢ to $1.05 a day. Any 20 percent increase in wages will be digested, but it will readily mean that a $400.00 rug will become a $500.00 rug at once. Some of the importing houses are predicting the end of oriental rugs from Iran in the next 10 years. These predictions have been made before but now the facts seem to justify this possibility.

The rare rugs that Americans accumulated for the past 70 years (and many of these were not rare at the time) will be scarcer and scarcer and become more valuable each year. The only places these are to be found are from the estates in America, and the Europeans will continue to haunt us.

I dislike building you up to buying with abandon lest you greatly overpay for some rug.

Only today an old customer of mine sent me a colored picture of a Ladik her son had bought (a rare type of Turkish prayer rug). It was immediately discerned that her son, thinking he had a great Ladik, had only bought one of the better ones made since World War II and not one of the valuable and rare Ladiks made well before 1900. If he paid $75.00 to $150.00, he has a semblance of a Ladik, though the border and much of the other design tell one it was one of the makeshift designs. But if he paid $800.00 to $2,000.00 for this Ladik he has been badly gypped. He had referred to my book and saw some Turkish plates of rare Ladiks and he judged this to be one. This rug was not true to any of the plates of any old Ladik. In buying a very rare rug the old saying, "A little knowledge is a dangerous thing" was never more applicable.

BOKHARAS FROM PAKISTAN

These strictly geometric design rugs in the traditional Tekke or Royal Bokhara design, with the name of Mori given them in Pakistan, are available today in great numbers in two qualities. The Karachi quality is a superior rug, fine, heavy, and one of the best rugs made in the last 70 years. The LaHore quality in the same general design, varies in quality. It is as finely woven or finer, but not as heavy and seldom has the worsted-like wool that the Karachi has. But they are indeed the finest woven rugs for the price that have been available for many years.

I am not going to predict what is going to happen to these rugs because I would have to predict what the Pakistani government will do in the way of subsidy. I think Russia plays a more important role at the moment than we do, but it is the American dollar for world trade that causes the government to subsidize the exportation of these. If the subsidy should be discontinued, these rugs would probably double in price overnight.

PERSIAN DESIGN RUGS FROM PAKISTAN

There is a good possibility that we will see the weavers in Pakistan start to produce large numbers of rather fine rugs in the Persian designs.

Several years ago I saw a great many of these in the London free port. I did not buy them because at that time they had copied only the Tabriz design. Evidently, they had bought many of the paper scale

Plate 26. ANTIQUE TURKISH PRAYER RUG. The inscription in Turkish, "God is perfect, praise be God," is repeated six times. It is believed that this rug was woven in Vienna, Austria at a time when the Turks occupied that city. The rug illustrates a very important point — that one cannot always give exact information on every rug. We have always agreed with the *Guide to the Collection of Carpets*, Victoria & Albert Museum, when it states time after time in describing Caucasian rugs, "The general term 'Caucasian' meets the difficulty presented by the frequent shifting of political boundaries in the past." That is so true of so many rugs. No expert can definitely place every rug such as this very rare old Turkish rug. Anyone who has seen the rarest Ghiordes, Kula, Ladik, Hereke, etc. will know that this is a very rare and wonderful old prayer rug. *(Courtesy of B. L. Garabedian, 276 Fifth Avenue, New York, N. Y.)*

Plate 27, above. JOSHIGAN from Iran. All of these have the same general pattern, a stylized or geometric floral design known by many different names, unchanged for two hundred years. The quality ranges from medium to very fine; the weave, shape, and colors determining the value. Size 10.7 × 14 feet.

Plate 28, below. SEMI-ANTIQUE AFSHAR (SHIRAZ) from Iran. This nomad tribal rug, with medium weave and medium but compact pile of virgin wool, is a moderate-priced rug of great durability for anyone seeking a geometric design to go with a Caucasian, or in place of Herez. Check for irregularities in shape and too much change of color. Most come in the same general design, in sizes ranging from 5 × 8 feet to 7.5 × 10.6 feet. This one measures 7.7 × 10.5 feet.

Plate 29, above. GUENSTEPEH from Iran. A new name in a heavy, good, average weave, with excellent wool quality. One of the most pleasing and durable rugs created in years. As durable as the best Kirman, Sarouk, or Kasvin. All are in the same general design as above. Background may be a bright flaming red instead of ivory. Size approximately 9×12 feet. *Plate 30, below.* QUM from Iran. One of the thinner, finely woven types of rugs being produced in Iran today in goodly numbers. About the same texture as a Kashan or new Ispahan. Though classed as finely woven, they vary greatly in weave, beauty of colors, design, wool quality, and price. Most are dozar sizes—about 6.5×4.5 feet. This specimen measures 7×4.5 feet.

Plate 31. EARLY KASVIN from Iran, employing designs usually found in Joshigan. The small angular bush form in triangle shape seldom appeared in any rug but Joshigan. This Kasvin is believed to have been woven in the town of Kasvin, instead of the city of Hamadan, where most present-day Kasvins are woven. The rug is thick and perfect, without flaws, even though it has been used in America for forty years and had considerable age when it was first imported. None of these are imported today because none are left in Iran. Any one of these found in an estate (and chances are remote you will find an old one in this design) is likely to have good nap, and very few, if any, of the defects listed in our check points. One of the choicest Kasvin carpets ever imported into America. Size 13 × 20 feet. *(Courtesy of Dr. and Mrs. John F. Lovejoy, Jacksonville, Florida)*

models of the Persian Tabriz, but they had done a rather poor job on most of these in that they had made the curvilinear line too angular and too set, and that gave them a machine-made-like appearance. I cannot predict it, but I hope these same people will use some of the Sarouk, Kirman, Kashan, and Hamadan designs.

In criticizing the Tabriz rugs, some of the finest rugs in the world are made in the town of Tabriz, but the majority are medium to rather coarse rugs. Why they discarded the lovely curvilinear design of 75 or more years ago, and produced these stiff machine-made-like designs, I do not know. I have noted in the last few years that some of these with ivory background are making some improvement in their designs.

RUGS FROM INDIA

In the preceding chapter we told you about the great increase in rug weaving in India, and that most of these rugs came in light colors and in Savonnerie and Chinese designs. At the present time, you can buy a 9×12 rug from India anywhere from $250.00 to about $850.00, depending on the fineness of weave and the wool quality. The present weaving wage in India is 28¢ a day as fixed by the government. This 28¢ a day in their money is not their lowest standard of living. With 400,000,000 people in India, I cannot see where the country can be industrialized enough and the standard of living raised to send these prices up very much in the next 10 years.

I would hope that they will again start weaving some of the fine rugs they used to produce in Persian design, such as Indo-Ispahan, Indo-Kashan, Indo-Sarouk, Indo-Feraghan, and others. This may fill the void that may develop from Iran.

I do predict that these rugs from India, with their simple designs, will have great appeal to the people who are making the change over from plain wall-to-wall to orientals. Once they observe their neighbors with one of these, and consider the durability of these rugs when compared to the average wall-to-wall rug, they will make the change. Rugs from India are sure to be in greater demand every year, and I think the price will stay down on these because India must have American dollars.

RUGS FROM COMMUNIST CHINA

If and when the American government recognizes this vast country and we resume trading with it, it is likely that a good number of

Chinese rugs will appear. If the prices of good ones are the same, or about the same, that we have seen in the London market, they will not be readily received or sold in great number because they will be too costly to produce volume. Whether the government there would subsidize them for export is another question. The duty or tariff on these will be 45 percent instead of the 18 percent from India. China would not come under the most favored nation clause, just as Russia does not. So the duty will be more than double. For my own projected taste I will still like the rugs from India in Chinese design better than those from China. Here I am assuming that the Chinese will go back to the old colors of the 1920 period when they were so popular, and not adopt the lighter and pastel colors that the rugs from India have.

RUGS FROM ROUMANIA

We have seen oriental rugs, all handmade, from Roumania. The quality, colors, and price are excellent, but the designs, for the most part, have the machine-made-like appearance that many of the Tabriz have and that the Turkish carpets (so-called Sparta and Anatolian) made right after World War I had.

The wool in these rugs coming from Roumania is superb—better than 9 out of 10 of the Persian rugs—so they will be very durable. We have liked one or two of the geometric designs and two or three of the Persian designs. The geometric designs do not have the domestic look, but the florals do. If they could improve the design and the government continues to subsidize them, these rugs could well find a big market in America.

IN CONCLUSION, one thing seems certain—that all choice antiques and semi-antiques in the rare category will continue to increase in price in America. This, because none of these types has been produced in 50 years, nor will they ever be produced again, and the price will depend on what the buyer is willing to pay. Prices for those that were bought in America have already reached a maximum in Europe, and the fantastic prices there are not, in my opinion, going to continue.

Chapter Ten

HISTORY OF GAMBLE IN BUYING ORIENTAL RUGS

HISTORY

Let's take a little time to review the different periods since about 1875 and to discuss the risk of each period. Beginning back before 1900, there was no American book on this subject. John Kimberly Mumford published his first book in 1900. It was a guide that all later writers followed. Up to that time the rugs that came had been made for the Orientals' own use. It was pretty much his every furnishing. They were not only his floor covering, but his bed, his partition, and his prayer rug. Baby hammocks were handwoven; tent bags were used in the place of sideboards and cabinets; saddlebags on donkeys and camels were the only means of carrying and moving belongings. These rugs were all woven for their own use, and while some were coarse nomad tribal rugs, others were much finer. The dyes and material in all were very good to excellent. These rugs were bought from the homes or the tribe and were perfect or only slightly worn. Whoever got them found that they lasted a lifetime. That is how oriental rugs got the reputation of wearing a lifetime. So, even if you bought one thin or slightly worn, you had a good rug. The chief fault in those days was that most of them would be somewhat irregular— seldom one perfectly straight. This did not seem to bother the early buyers of oriental rugs as it does many people today, and the other fault was that there would be many shadings and changes of color which is not a real fault unless it mars the beauty of the rug. So, there was no real danger in those days, except that of overpaying and exaggeration as to the merits of the rug.

Mr. Mumford willed all of his books and writings to me. In one of his lectures, given about 1915, he tells this cute story.

"So little was known about oriental rugs in those days that the man who had a few to dispose of was safe in telling almost any 'whopper' he pleased. There was nobody with knowledge enough to contradict him. So they fell into the habit of gorgeous exaggeration and they seem never to have gotten cured of it."

"There was a man among those early venders—and unlike Ananias and Sapphiro he is still alive—who had a rug that he was trying to to sell to a very cautions and skeptical old lady. She was safeguarding herself with a great many questions. 'Young man,' she said, 'will this thing fade?'

" 'Madam' he replied, 'the most wonderful thing about these magnificent rugs is the color. It isn't like any other color in the world. You have sheep here in America. They are all white, or brown, or black. In my country, where these rugs are made, it is altogether different. The sheep of Asia are of every color of the rainbow. Purple, blue, green, yellow and red—every color you can think of. Why, madam, believe me, when you see a flock of them all together it is like the sunset sky. They make the whole hillside look like a kaleidoscope. When they are sheared all they have to do is sort out the wool and the weaver picks out whatever colors he wants for the rugs. No, madam, these colors can *never* fade, because they were *born* fast.'

" 'Dear me,' she said, 'how remarkable.' "

ANILINE DYES

The next period was the "Aniline Dyes" scare period. You find Mr. Mumford's book and the books up to 1917 warning everyone against the German aniline dyes. They warned that colors would bleed, that they were harsh, and also that the colors would fade out.

This fear was exaggerated even though it is true that German merchants did come to Persia, and did sell to the weavers German aniline dyes. And many weavers did use these cheap dyes rather than take the trouble of obtaining their vegetable dyes which often was a long process.

Since these books were the main reference in every library from 1900 to 1950, and up to a few years ago, it was not surprising that hundreds of people inquired and wanted some assurance that the rug had vegetable dyes. By 1924 this aniline dye question was of little importance to anyone. By that time the limited number of rugs that had been made with aniline dyes around 1895 to 1910 had disappeared, or whenever one came into a dealer's hand or came from Persia in a group, it was unmistakable and I would say that the risk was not one in a thousand rugs in 1924. And yet for 30 years thereafter and up to a few years ago, anyone who went to the library to learn something about oriental rugs, after reading all the old books had one fear "aniline dyes."

When the greater evil appeared that we now discuss, it was a ten times greater hazard, to my mind, than the fear of aniline dyes. People continued to ask about this point when they should have been asking whether the rug was chemically washed and painted. The standard books had been written before this process became so general. I neglected one very important point. The small Turkish mats, prayer rugs, and scatter rugs woven in Turkey after World War I, did use aniline dyes and they were horrible examples of small oriental rugs. In sizes approximately 2×3 ft., 3×5 ft., and 4×6 ft. These sold for the most part from $19.00 to $49.00. The small mats sold for $2.00 to $10.00. They, too, are no longer a problem because practically everyone of them has been worn out and discarded, and the few that might appear are going to have little appeal to the general public. The mass of rugs woven in Turkey at that time in carpet sizes using Persian designs, employed good dyes instead of the aniline.

THE CHEMICAL TREATMENT OF RUGS

The worst period, and to my mind the worse thing that could happen to oriental rugs, was the chemical washing and painting process that prevailed pretty generally from 1905 to 1955. Most dealers and practically every department store that sold oriental rugs sold these, and would not agree with me.

My large book had a detailed chapter on this subject. (We also have a free booklet of this chapter.) The principal idea, or in simplest terms, treatment means the application of chloride of lime, chlorine peroxide or hydrogen, oxalic, and sulphuric acid, or some other chemical, the purpose being to reduce the harsh colors of the new fabric. The creation of artificial sheen is also a part of the treatment process. I will not go into this in great detail because if you have my book it is completely covered. If not, we will gladly send you free of charge a booklet on this process. My objection was that it not only removed a lot of nap initially, but it damaged the remaining nap and after the treatment it was generally necessary to have these touched to kill the very faded look. Then with an application of glycerine or paraffin wax under hot rollers, a beautiful sheen appeared. That sheen was not permanent.

This chemical treatment of rugs was not an occasional thing or one that was done on a rug every now and then. It was the general rule, and from 1905 to 1955, 95% or more of all Sarouks sold in America were both chemically washed and painted. You could not sell these to a collector or a person who had read the least bit on the subject of oriental rugs. Very definitely, seven out of ten rugs sold during that period were so treated. People continually tell me, "My parents' Sarouk was bought over 40 years ago, so it is not treated." But that was when the procedure was so general. The great stores even advertised beautifully washed oriental rugs. The old books (the only books on the subject in the libraries) did not warn the public sufficiently against this treatment. Mr. A. U. Dilley, in his first little book published in 1909 criticized it only slightly, but he did say very emphatically that people who loved antique rugs maintained that the treatment process was a fraud. Mr. Walter Hawley, in his book, did not discourage this and noted only a mild criticism.

For 45 years I have written hundreds of articles against this process and boast that I have never sold a rug so treated. I wonder if there is any other dealer in America who can make such a boast even though I know a limited number of them do not like the chemical washing.

The proof of the pudding is now clear. The average chemically washed and painted rug wore out in a short time and if later washed in soap and water, often became muddy looking. The finest chemically washed and painted rugs went on to wear 25 to 30 years, and even longer, but at the end of that time they began to show some fading and some wear, if not being well-worn. They have very little value today. The person who bought an inexpensive, chemically washed oriental rug in 1924–30, discarded that rug 15 or 20 years later, or, at least, it is a sick affair. Those who bought the high-priced washed Sarouks, and washed Kashans, and other high quality rugs, found they lasted the 25 years as stated, but they were beginning to lose or had lost much of their nap as well as their beauty, and most of their value.

On the other hand, the person who bought a bright new Sarouk or Kashan, or even a good heavy quality Hamadan, Ingelas or what not, generally has a good rug today—40 years later. They have a rug that is quite salable and, as a rule, worth much more than when they bought it. Even if the rug is somewhat thin, this is true. But the person who paid good money for one of the chemically washed and painted ones finds that they can secure very little money or very little in exchange for it.

Oftentimes a chemically washed 9×12 Sarouk sold for $100.00 to $250.00. Now, if they had bought even a bright new Sarouk, even after all these years it would be mellow and more beautiful and most likely show little wear. Generally they can get twice to several times as much as they paid for it. Most big stores did not hesitate to tell you that the rugs were chemically washed and painted if you asked them. But over the course of years, I have run into many cases where the dealer had told his customer that the chemically washed and painted rug was a real antique, and had denied that it was washed and painted. That probably was the exception. The fact was that every large store that sold oriental rugs sold them; your favorite department store sold them and 95 out of 100 dealers sold them.

They would be selling them today if the labor cost had not made the process prohibitive, except in the must cases. Must cases being where the rug is so discolored from light washing, or is unsalable unless something is done to improve its looks.

Even this 50 year period—1905–1955—of chemical washing was not as dangerous to the layman as today's situation.

PRESENT-DAY PITFALLS

At no time in the past 75 years have the odds been so against the layman.

At no time in history has the merchandising and advertising of orientals reached such a low unethical level, and at no time have so many of the new Persian rugs come in with so many faults. Some of these faults can be corrected completely, but a very big percentage of them have faults that detract greatly from the value of the rug. The risk today is truly great and I quickly add, "Go to a good dealer and you can usually find an excellent rug." You can buy the excellent rug of the same type as you will find a poorer one of the type and size at an auction or used rug sale. You will pay no more for the excellent rug. With the good roads and automobiles, these itinerant auctioneers roam the country and make one to three day stands, and the sucker who buys these rugs has no recourse from the itinerant auctioneer.

Perhaps the many great name stores using the used rug sale gimmick produce the biggest gamble of all. Hardly a one of these will buy or take in trade a used rug. We have already discussed this in detail. Thousands of people are buying worn out rugs with areas that have been painted, and at ridiculously high prices in many cases. It is the ad that produces the big volume and these merchandise managers have their jobs at stake for volume. But why the heads of stores are so blind as to permit the continuance of these used rug sales is beyond me. There is no jealousy on my part, or any good dealer's part, because it only brings us much more business that we would not otherwise have.

If the danger was great in the chemically washed and painted period, it is much greater today because thousands of these used chemically washed and painted rugs are offered on these used rug sales at fancy prices, and they are only listed as used rugs. Seldom does the salesman point this out to you.

HIGHWAY ROBBERY

Ignorance on the part of the head of the department, and stupidity on the part of the merchandise manager, and crookedness by exorbitant prices on the part of the itinerant dealer who runs the sale, or by the manager of the department who has no license to spend money for any store, is found in many advertisements by stores which do not have a permanent oriental rug department.

Yes, there are a lot of crooks, liars, and cheats still abroad. I have resisted taking my gloves off, but lately I have had a number of ads sent to me by old customers and I fear that some of these old established stores are presenting as big a gamble as any auction or "Used Rug Sale."

I have in hand an ad by a department store far removed from competition in a town of about 50,000 people. The ad says "33 to 50% off regular price." Right off they have listed in the ad a Hamadan rug 2×3, regular $50.00 for $24.95. I do not recall in my 46 years a 2×3 Hamadan being priced *regularly* $25.00, much less $50.00. Whether sale or regular, $15.00 to $19.00 has been the price of these Hamadan mats up to the present time. Next, a 2×3 Sarouk mat is listed $83.00 regular, sale $54.95. Most any store will offer you one maximum $35.00 regular price, sale $29.00 to $33.00—some qualities for less. Next a 2×4 Sarouk rug, regular $150.00, sale $99.95. Not in 46 years has one of these been $100.00 at regular prices, much less $150.00. Today's price should be maximum $69.00—some for less. Then the next item a 12.3×9.7 ft. Herez, regular $1350.00, sale $899.00. Now,

164

Plate 32. ANTIQUE SAVONNERIE from Austria. One of the rarest designs, believed to have been woven in Czechoslovakia or Austria, where many of the Savonneries were woven. This specimen originally came from a Russian palace. Rug was originally much larger, but was reduced in size thirty-eight years ago for Colonel Jacobsen's own home. Now in the dining room of the Mary Washington Home, Fredericksburg, Virginia. Donated by Charles W. Jacobsen, Inc. Size approxirnately 14.8 × 17.6 feet. *(Courtesy of the Mary Washington Branch, A.P.V.A.)*

Plate 33, above. ANTIQUE SILK SAMARKAND from Central Asia. In bedroom of the Mary Washington Home (mother of George Washington) in Fredericksburg, Virginia. A very old and extremely rare Samarkand. Rug is worn thin and has had considerable repairs at one end. Nevertheless, because of its suitability for this home, being of the same or, more probably, an older period, and having the typical design and characteristics of a very old and noteworthy Samarkand, one must overlook the usual check points for defects. Donated by Mrs. Donald McKinnery, Cherry Hill, New Jersey, in memory of her husband. Size 13.4×6.6 feet. Plate 34, below. RARE ANTIQUE BAKU from Caucasia. In bedroom of the Mary Washington Home, Fredericksburg, Virginia. Typical Baku design with angular floriated pears. One of the earliest and best examples of this type. Rug is quite thin, but still very valuable. If in better condition it would be priceless. Donated by Mr. and Mrs. C. D. Jensen, Weathersfield, Connecticut. Size 12.8×6.1 feet. (Courtesy of the Mary Washington Branch, A.P.V.A.)

Plate 35, above. OLD ISPAHAN FROM IRAN. In the study of Mr. and Mrs. Levin Houston's home in Fredericksburg, Virginia. Size 10.7×7.4 feet. *Plate 36, right.* OLD FERAGHAN from Iran, with Gula Henna design. In the hall of Mr. and Mrs. Levin Houston's home in Fredericksburg, Virginia. Size 6.6×4.6 feet. A magnificent book of colored plates and descriptions could well be made of the rare and lovely early American furnishings in this home, the Mary Washington Home, and the Rising Sun Tavern in Fredericksburg.

Plate 37. ANTIQUE OUSHAK from Turkey. In the Great Room of the Rising Sun Tavern (home of George Washington's brother) in Fredericksburg, Virginia. A very old rug, perhaps as old as the Tavern itself, with designs found in so many of the old master's paintings of the period. Check point for defect in changes in color should be ignored in a rug of this period. Donated by Mrs. Howard Will, Syracuse, New York. Size approximately 12 × 12 feet. *(Courtesy of the Mary Washington Branch, A.P.V.A.)*

I have sold perhaps 100,000 Herez rugs. I have never sold the rarest antique in this size as high as $899.00, and the statement of $1350.00 regular price is ridiculous. How amusing this ad is to any dealer with any competition.

I could list all of them. Then they add, "IF YOU HAVE EVER DREAMED OF OWNING GENUINE ORIENTALS HERE'S THE OPPORTUNITY OF A LIFETIME."

Now, how do you analyze such an ad? Why do we say the gamble is greater today?

First, the president of this store is asleep on the job by allowing such prices to be advertised. The same is true, and more so, of his merchandise manager. I do not know whether this is a sale put on by an itinerant salesman who pays them a commission, and rightly so, or whether some smart operator in New York has given them these rugs on consignment at ridiculously high prices and all this store knows is to accept the names and take their cost and add 50 to 100%. There is no other explanation. But I know this store and it has been a reliable store for the past 50 years. Then why such an ad?

I recall ten years ago when I was furnishing a close relative in Savannah, Georgia, some rugs to sell. At that time we had certain items that cost $65.00 that we were offering for $98.00 to $100.00. I was amazed to walk into a good furniture store there and find that they had some 20 rugs shipped to them from New York on approval. These same 5×3 rugs were priced at $195.00. When I talked to the manager of the department, who hardly knew one rug from the other, he told me the rugs had been sent them on consignment for $100.00 to $120.00. So the importer was making a sucker out of him, as he could have bought the same for much less.

In conclusion there is no way to eliminate gullibility, no way to eliminate the person who is trying to get something for nothing, and, since it is also difficult to eliminate the sharp traders and crooks in the business, there is no way to help this class. Those who take the time to read a little, to make some comparison as to price, and use a little good horse sense, are going to continue to get good rugs and good values.

Chapter Eleven
CARE OF ORIENTAL RUGS

In my large book, *Oriental Rugs—A Complete Guide,* I covered this subject as well as space permitted in Chapter Twenty-One.

We find that housewives are very timid in following directions for cleaning their rugs at home. I want to add to what I said at that time and go into such details that they will no longer hesitate to sponge their rugs themselves, if they don't have a big son or domestic help to do it.

We are still asked about electric vacuum cleaners. Again, we say, use the one of your choice once or twice a week. It will do no harm to any average oriental rug, or even to a very poor one. If the rug happens to be chemically treated, then I would modify this and say use the electric cleaner with a brush not more than once a week. It may do some little harm over the years, but you are still going to use one.

One good suggestion is to turn your rugs upside down at least once a year and vacuum the rug from the back. No matter how good a housekeeper you are, you will likely sweep up a quart or more of dust, sand and grit. And of course you will then want to vacuum it on the right side.

MOTHPROOFING AND DE-MOTHING

There is no excuse for an oriental rug ever being motheaten today. There are excellent moth preventives—100 percent sure if used once a year. I made the mistake of mentioning the product "Keyspray" in my large book, a moth spray material that we have used for many years. The company that made this has since sold out to the Texize Chemicals, Inc. of Greenville, S. C., and the name of this mothproofing material has been changed to "Sect-O-Cide." This is the same company that sells "K 2r Spot-Lifter." You probably cannot do better in protecting your rugs than with this Sect-O-Cide, but there are other sprays made by the different oil companies, and they are less expensive. Most of these do not have the cehmical contents that Sect-O-Cide has and most of these have more odor than this Sect-O-Cide.

An application of this on the underside of the rug along the outer edge, i. e. spraying a band one to three ft. wide on a large rug on the reverse side, is sufficient to prevent moth damage. Use care not to get this on your sponge-rubber cushion as the solvent will soften or melt the rubber. That is the only care required. Too little or soaking the rug wet with the liquid will do no harm. Rubbed on with a cloth wet with the liquid spray will be just as good as spraying it on. But again, the rug should not be laid back on the rubber pad for a few minutes to half an hour.

Spray, or rub with a cloth, the nap surface which is under furniture. If you want to do a 100 percent job, and it will take only a few minutes to cover the entire rug instead of just spraying under the furniture, then cover the entire nap surface with the spray material.

In addition to mothproofing, this gives the rug a fresh look. We spray every rug we sell or ship out on approval, covering the entire nap surface with this Sect-O-Cide. Spray and then sweep with a regular house broom and you will be amazed at the clean and fresh look it gives a rug.

A thorough soaking with this material or any solvent will de-moth the rug and destroy the moth eggs, worms, or larvae, and also moth-proof the rug for at least a year. If you discover moth eggs or larvae or moth worms in only one small section of the rug, a soaking of this section so that the rug in that area is wet right thru to the back, will completely de-moth the rug.

CLEANING YOUR RUG AT HOME

But the main subject I wish to cover here is the washing of your valuable rugs. For many years, when one asked me how often they should have their oriental rugs sent out to professional cleaners to be washed (with soap and water), my stock answer has been, "When the rug is dirty." Don't have it cleaned every year unless you want to destroy the rug in a few years. SPONGE IT AT HOME AS OFTEN AS YOU WISH, AT LEAST ONCE A YEAR; AND ONCE A MONTH WILL DO NO HARM IF YOUR HOME REQUIRES

IT ALTHOUGH THAT WILL SELDOM BE NECESSARY.

Many years ago, I advised having rugs cleaned every three to five years. With the high cost of labor and equipment in recent years, I have changed my ideas on this, and 45 years' experience and observation influences my change of position.

My advice is to send your rugs out to the so-called professional cleaners only when your rugs are very dirty and beyond home cleaning. And I would do more than look in the yellow pages for the largest advertisers for rug cleaning. If you do good home cleaning with the present-day soaps especially designed for this, you will not need to send your rugs out to be cleaned for many years.

If you are not up to doing the washing in the home yourself, the procedure is so simple and so safe that if your cleaning woman will not do it, then any ordinary day laborer can, and certainly a son 12 years of age or older can do a good job in one hour on quite a large rug.

You can do a good job and a safer job than having the so-called professional cleaners come in and clean your rugs in your home. They do not soap and water clean your rugs in your home but merely shampoo them with soap suds or clean with powder. I am simply saying that with certain oil based soaps you can do just about as good a job and to my mind a far safer job. You should use a sponge or a hand brush to scrub the rug. Most of the professionals will use a rotating brush (often with hard bristles) that usually does little or no harm, but which can do a lot of harm in the hands of a careless or inexperienced employee of the company.

The hand sponging is foolproof. We are still using the same general type soap, supposedly the same "Marvella," but now sold under the name of "Premium Soap" and manufactured and sold by the Texize Company of Greenville, S. C. Stores, clubs, and dealers can order this directly from this company. We buy it in large 50 gallon drums. They probably have it in 5 gallon drums. One cup of this mixed with 25 cups of water will clean 2 or 3 rugs size 9×12 ft. At home we mix $\frac{1}{2}$ cup of soap with 12 cups of water. I hope they will put it out in gallon containers. If you can't buy it, we can furnish about a gallon. Do not be timid about trying this. There is not the slightest risk. Too much soap, or too little, or too much water in the sponge is not going to harm the rug. It takes perhaps an hour to dry. The worst you can do is to not clean the rug as perfectly as you hoped.

Take a synthetic sponge (this is best) and dip it in the soap-and-water solution. Then squeeze much of the water out and rub or scrub the rug in the easiest manner. Up and down the rug, crosswise, or use a circular motion; any one or a combination of these will give results. I personally like to lay the nap in one direction after cleaning a small area. You will quickly see in which direction you need to make the last few strokes to accomplish this. This is not essential. If the rug is real dirty you can use more water and not just the lather. It will take a little longer to dry, but there is no danger of the water going through to the padding or the floor. But using just the suds after squeezing out the water will usually be sufficient.

If you have turned the rug upside down and vacuumed the back and removed the dust and grit, you will have a good job when you sponge it. You don't have to do this every time you want to sponge the rug off, but it should be done at least once a year.

To clean the fringes you need to get some heavy paper or plastic material to lay under the end of the rug and about a foot beyond the fringe. Having the paper in place, you simply scrub the fringe with sponge or brush—perhaps a hand brush is better. Remove the water with the sponge or with flat side of a board, or even with the edge of the brush. When dry, you brush it out and trim the tip ends even with a pair of scissors.

PROFESSIONAL RUG CLEANERS

Now, I did not mean to rule the professional rug cleaner entirely out of the picture. Certainly when the rugs are very dirty you must send them out to be cleaned—for a real washing and a thorough rinsing. Note, I say a thorough rinsing. Most cleaning plants around the country merely shampoo the rug with suds and soap and do not rinse.

I present this long discourse on sponging or cleaning at home because I think you can do as good a job as these cleaners, and perhaps a safer job, and at a fraction of the cost. So check up on the cleaning plant to which you send your valuable rugs.

One other reason why I do not approve of sending your rugs out every year or two is the difficulty of properly cleaning the fringe. It is most difficult for the cleaner to keep the rugs he washes from having the fringe turn brown in the drying room. And it is very nearly impossible to prevent this. When there is a small amount of soap left in the rug and it gets on the fringe, the heat serves to turn the white cotton fringe brown. I had trouble with this for many years and never did solve it completely. When the rug comes out of the drying room with brown fringes there is only one thing to do, and that is to use a light bleach. Doing this too many times rots the fringe.

An up-to-date drying room is supposed to have the air changed every few minutes, so that the fringe does not brown. But it is most difficult to have this under perfect control.

If I had a plant in Florida or the South, I would wash and rinse every rug and then put them out in the open fresh air to dry. This would take quite a trolley line to run them in and out on bright sunny days. It would also mean that you would not wash on cloudy or rainy days. THIS WOULD BE THE BEST THOROUGH CLEANING JOB I CAN IMAGINE.

So once again, remember you can do a good cleaning job in your home; and if you keep the rugs clean, whether this means sponging them once a year or once every three months, you may not need to send your rugs to the cleaners in twenty years.

Here in Florida, where I am punching out this book on my portable, we have the light-colored Savonneries, shown in this book on page 17. Both rugs are Savonneries in the same exact colors and design. The rug in the living room has been down for eight years and has just been sponged by my lovely wife (old lazy me) for the first time. Now, the same rug in the dining room is sponged at least every three months to remove small food stains. (Yes, the old man is the guilty one.) K 2r Spot Remover or Goddard will easily remove any grease spots from this plain field and not leave a ring.

Now, there are other soaps but, in our opinion, none more satisfactory than this soap that we use. We have tried many and they are satisfactory, but my officers and employees still insist that Premium Soap (formerly called Marvella) is the best. Of course, I believe there must be others just as good.

The Johnson Wax people have just come out with one they called "Glory." I had one of my men clean some rugs in our store with this as an experiment, and it was good. We stick, however, to our old one. Perhaps my people are prejudiced because they have used it so satisfactorily for so many years. And the cost of this is so little; a dollar's worth will clean some three 9×12 ft. rugs.

REMOVAL OF SPOTS

Certain types of spots on a rug can be removed without cleaning the whole rug. If the spot is grease, there are a number of spot removers that will remove the spot and not leave a ring. K 2r by the Texize Company (most stores carry this) and Goddards spot remover also is excellent for removing grease spots. No doubt, there are others that will do this same job.

You can also generally remove these by sponging them away with a number of excellent rug soaps. The only problem here is that if you scrub too hard in one area you may have to sponge the entire rug. But it is no real effort to sponge the entire rug, say a 9×12 ft. rug, in 15 to 30 minutes.

I am not going to try to tell you how to take care of all spots or accidents to oriental rugs. There are many small publications on spot removers. Spilling food causes no real damage and presents no great problem to remove. Usually, sponging with the soaps we mention or other good soaps, will remove food spots.

Try a cloth or sponge with plain cold water first. This is especially effective with coffee spots. Quickly sponge it out with cold water. Worse than coffee are some of the charged water drinks—soft drinks, etc. It is necessary to get plain water on these quickly or as soon as discovered, otherwise they will create faded spots. After using plain water it is well to use the soap and sponge off as already described.

One of the worse stains to remove is dog urine. Any type is bad but some types are worse than others. Again sponging with plain water as soon as detected will eliminate damage. Many such stains, if not re-moved, can destroy much of the value of the rug. These are ten times more dangerous to plain wall-to-wall carpet than to any type of oriental. Actually, small stains on a figured oriental aren't going to be readily noticed.

But please note I don't want to appear prejudiced against the "best friend a man ever had." I have always maintained that oriental rugs are compatible with pets in the home. I certainly would not want to see them not have the full run of the house.

Nevertheless we have seen a very few tragic cases: one where a dog had used the huge Kirman hundreds of times (in fact, my guess is he habitually used the rug). There is no excuse for such a situation.

I want to tell you about one experiment I made. We took in trade a large Savonnerie from India with open plain ivory field, the only design in the rug being in the border (our Design 9612-B as shown on page 17). Our salesman making the transaction did not take the time to look under a coffee table and other furniture. (He failed to heed our warning under "Check Points on Buying a Used Rug.") Once in our store we found a dozen large, discolored areas (dog stains). We sponged this rug several times but the stains had been there too long. My service people gave up on removing them. We simply had made a bad mistake and were about to lose several hundred dollars. I had this huge rug (12×20 ft.) unrolled and sprayed with the K 2 r Spot Remover. At first it did not seem to be removing these stains. But over the course of a month these spots were sprayed several times with the K 2r and each time we simply rolled it back up without removing the dried white powder. Finally, the dog spots were completely eliminated.

I do not promise that you will have this same success. K 2r is sold as a grease-spot remover. But I suggest you try this procedure provided you will not write me if it does not work as well.

Ink spots seldom happen, but large ones can be serious. Our method is to pour milk immediately on the area and scoop it up with a tablespoon. You will get most of it out. Then sponge with soap and water. If not completely removed send it to a professional cleaner if you know a good one.

Small cigarette burns are not serious and the spots can be rewoven quickly and inexpensively. Large burned areas, however, can be rewoven only at considerable expense.

Chapter Twelve

CLASSIFICATION AND RESUME

My large book, *Oriental Rugs—A Complete Guide* covers this subject in considerable detail. In hope that each reader of this new book has the large book at hand. Appreciating the fact that many people will come upon this, my latest and last effort at book writing, before they learn about the larger edition which, as a whole, is very different from the material presented here, I am going to repeat much of that information on "Classification of Oriental Rugs," and also, add some new thoughts on this subject that might help beginners in buying their first rugs.

CLASSIFICATION BY COUNTRIES

Rugs are grouped according to the country in which they are made. We refer to the country as the family of the rug. The specific name usually means, or rather meant, the town or district in which it was made. Thus we should say Kirman is the name of a fine rug from Iran.

Other rugs, like most of the rugs from India, are given trade names by the company that makes them, or even by the American importer, as my company does with our own importation of these.

Here is a complete list, with the exception of a few small countries that produce a mere handful of unimportant rugs for their own use. Some of these countries are not weaving or, at least, not exporting rugs today. This list is of countries that have woven in the past 50 years. Iran (formerly called Persia), India, Pakistan, and Afghanistan, are the principal producers, and the dollar-wise volume of their output is in the order shown.

1. Iran (Persia)   3. Pakistan   5. Japan
2. India   4. Afghanistan

179

6. Balkan rugs—hand woven in Bulgaria and Roumania
7. Caucasia—now several Soviet States (none imported today)
8. Turkey (none imported today)
9. China (none imported today)
10. Turkestan or Turkoman group—also called Central Asiatic group (now Soviet States) (none imported today)
11. Greece (made only during period 1923–1931) (none imported today)

CLASSIFICATION ACCORDING TO AGE

New rugs
Semi-antique or semi-old rugs
Antique rugs
Used rugs

We can make many classifications of new rugs, the two most important being those using the same traditional designs that were used many years ago—as opposed to some newly developed designs—namely, the Sarouks and the Kirmans from Iran. Both types include rugs in newly created designs and also in traditional designs.

Antique rugs may be further classified as, RARE ANTIQUE RUGS, which would be collectors' or museum qualities, and practical antique rugs, or just antique rugs. This last means a good average rug that qualifies as to age, but which is NOT CHOICE ENOUGH OR RARE ENOUGH TO BE A REAL OBJECT OF ART. A collector would not be interested in these even though they are beautiful utility old rugs.

The term USED RUGS can include antiques and semi-antiques, but we do not class choice antiques or semi-antiques as USED.

Another classification can be made according to sizes, and I shall not give you the old Persian names that indicated sizes, such as pushti—which means a small mat—but just tell you that in America we refer to these as being rugs if they are scatter sizes. Any oriental about 5×8 ft. or smaller is also referred to as a rug; and any rug approximately 6×9 ft. and larger is called a carpet in America.

In Europe they refer to all oriental rugs as carpets, regardless of the size.

HERE IS A LIST OF MOST OF THE PERSIAN NAMES. Some few villages and technical sub-divisions under these names are not attempted.

*Indicates that these are not being woven today, and are seldom available even from estates. All are pretty much in the hands of collectors.

Abedeh
Afshar (Afshari)
Ahar
Ainabad
Arak (Arac)
Ardabil
Bahktiari
Bashkshis (Bakshaish)
Baluchistan (Beloochistan)
Bibikabad
Bijar
Birjand
Borchalu
Dargazine
Feraghan *
Gorevan
Guenstepeh
Hamadan
Herat *
Herez (Heriz)
Hosseinabad
Ingelas
Ispahan
Ispahan Meshed
Josan
Joshigan
Kashan (Keshan)
Kasvin (Kazvin)
Karadagh *
Karaja
Karaje *
Kaputarhang
Khanabad
Kirman (Kerman)
Kirmanshah (Kermanshah) *
Khorasan (Khursan)

Kurdistan
Lillihan
Mahal
Mecca Shiraz (Qashqai)
Melayer *
Meshed
Mehreban
Mir-Sarabend
Mosul
Muskabad
Nain
Niris
Polonaise *
Qashgai (Kashai) (Ghasgai)
Qum (Qom) (Gum)
Ramishan
Sarabend
Savalan
Sarouk (Saruk)
Sena (Senna) (Senneh) *
Sena-Kelim *
Sena-Kurd
Serapi *
Serab
Shiraz
Suj-Bulak *
Sultanabad
Tabriz
Tajabad
Tarfish
Teheran (Tehran)
Turkbaff (Turkibaff)
Veramin *
Yezd
Zanjan
Zeli-Sultan *

I had not intended printing this list since it is in my large book, but for those who happen to have this volume only, it will be helpful. Also, we have added below code numbers that give a comparative price range so that you may know which are the most expensive and which cost less. The number listed, for example 15, does not mean $15.00 or $150.00. It is just a basis of comparison with other named rugs. Each unit could mean $30.00 or it could mean $20.00. It is just a method of comparing values.

When you read that long list of names of rugs from Iran, you must not get the idea that these rugs are available in all sizes. Different rugs are made in different sizes.

CLASSIFICATION OF 9 × 12 FT. RUGS

When you go into a store seeking a 9 × 12 ft. Persian rug, you will be amazed at how comparatively few of the many types make large rugs. This is due mainly to the fact that many of the homes in outlying districts in Iran do not have looms wide enough to weave a 9 × 12 ft. rug. Nor do they have the experience or tradition in weaving large rugs.

In order that you may have some basis for comparison of value on some new rugs, following is a list of unit numbers which are given only to enable you to make or have some idea as to the relative value of these rugs. For instance, the number 15 units is given only for comparative prices. It could mean $15.00 per sq. ft. for the rug. Thus, if a rug is exactly 9 × 12 ft., it would have 108 sq. ft., and at $15.00 per sq. ft., it would cost $1,620.00. Likewise, say a Bibikabad at $4.50 per sq. ft. would be $486.00.. It is intended only to give a comparative valuation between the different types. You would perhaps find it easier to use this unit as so many dollars per sq. ft. The value of the unit will no doubt change in the next few years. These comparative prices refer to new rugs, and not to old and antique rugs.

Kirman	(80/40 qualities)	—	12–15 units
Kashan	(better qualities)	—	12–17 ,,
Sarouk	(average to best)	—	$8\frac{1}{2}$–12 ,,
Sarabend Sarouk		—	$9\frac{1}{2}$–11 ,,
Sarouk	(classical)	—	10–15 ,,
Qum (Gum)	(rarely available as large as 9 × 12 ft.)	—	11–17 ,,

Tabriz	(finer quality)	—	12–16	,,
Joshigan	(average to best)	—	$6\frac{1}{2}$–11	,,
Kasvin	(average to best)	—	$7\frac{1}{2}$–11	,,
Ingelas		—	6–$8\frac{1}{2}$	,,
Herez	(better qualities)	—	$5\frac{1}{2}$–$7\frac{1}{2}$	,,
Gorevan		—	4–6	,,
Kirman, Bazaar Quality		—	$6\frac{1}{2}$—9	,,
	(better quality)			
Tabriz, Bazaar Quality		—	5–9	,,
	(average to good)			
Hosseinabad		—	$5\frac{1}{2}$–8	,,
Arak (real Arak)		—	5–$8\frac{1}{2}$	,,
Sultanabad	(better qualities)	—	4–6	,,
Mahal		—	$3\frac{1}{2}$–6	,,
Meshed	(better qualities)	—	$5\frac{1}{2}$–8	,,
Ispahan Meshed	(better qualities)	—	7–12	,,
Aroon	(coarser Kashan)	—	6–9	,,
Bibikabad	(contract quality)	—	$5\frac{1}{2}$–$8\frac{1}{2}$	,,
Bibikabad	(family made)	—	$4\frac{1}{2}$–$5\frac{1}{2}$	,,
Kaputarhang		—	4–5	,,
Ramishan		—	$5\frac{1}{2}$–$7\frac{1}{2}$	,,
Guenstepeh		—	7–9	,,

The comparative price unit is given on the assumption that the rug is a good one of its type, and not one of the poorest of its type. Occasionally, we buy a few coarser Sarouks because they are thick and rather good-looking, even though not first quality. The unit cost could be about 8.

0 1 2 3 4 5 6 7 8 9

Figure 9. Dated rugs. Sometimes a rug has the date recorded in Arabic number woven in the rug. These represent the Mohammedan year, dating from the time of the Hegira (July 622). The lunar and not the solar year is used in the Moslem chronology. The lunar year gains about one year in every 33.7 years, making it rather complicated to figure out the Christian year. Assuming the date woven into the rug is 1247, our date would be 1247 less 37 (1210) plus 622, or 1832. You arrive at the 37 figure by dividing 1247 by 33.7.

183

Actually, when you walk into a store which has a rather large stock of oriental rugs, you are not going to find all of these types in the 9×12 ft. size. Usually, not more than 6 or 8 different types, such as the following:

Kirman	80–40 quality
Sarouk	(red or rose allover design)
Bibikabad	(in two qualities)
Herez	(different qualities of Gorevans, Herez and others from districts such as Ahar, Mihriban, Bahkshish, etc., will be offered as Herez. All have same general design.)

Sarabend Sarouk
Kasvin
Kaputarhang
Guenstepeh
Kashan
Mahal
Arak

These last two have the same general characteristics—Arak being the better rug.

There is a good chance that the store may have a Joshigan, a Meshed, a medium quality Tabriz, an Ingelas, or a Hosseinabad. (Very few of the last two made in this size.)

WHILE WE ARE TALKING ABOUT CLASSIFICATION as to sizes, and have covered available 9×12 ft. sizes, we should add that the only other 9×12 ft. size rugs in the deeper or typical old oriental designs are the Bokhara types from PAKISTAN and AFGHANISTAN. In Pakistan they are known as Mori. Most stores should be able to offer you one of the LaHore qualities at a reasonable price.

Bokhara (LaHore quality)	—	4–$7\frac{1}{2}$ Units
Bokhara (Karachi quality)	—	8–12 ,,

Both are made in a number of colors, but most will have the wine red field. All are in the old Tekke (Royal Bokhara design) and a few with the rare Salor Bokhara design.

CARPET SIZES LARGER THAN 9×12 FT.

When you seek a size larger than 9×12 ft. you will, or can, find a good selection in sizes approximately 10×14 ft. in most of the types listed under 9×12 ft. sizes, and at the same comparative prices.

Plate 38. SEMI-ANTIQUE KASHAN from Iran. One of the loveliest designs with an open field to be found in Kashans, one of the best woven in Iran, and one of the most popular among the Persians themselves. Rug is shown to illustrate some bad changes of color. Changes like this in a plain field that are gradual are not objectionable, but radical changes in a new or semi-antique rug like this would definitely be objectionable to most people and make the rug considerably less valuable.

BUT IF YOU SEEK A PERSIAN CARPET LARGER THAN THE 10×14 FT. SIZE, you will find a tremendous shortage in the larger size carpet; the exception being in the excellent contract-quality Kirman, the Kasvin, and the Bibikabad. Sarouks once plentiful in the large sizes are scarce and at a premium. Not very many of the Sarabend Sarouks or the classical design Sarouks are made in sizes larger than 10×14 ft.

Once there was a great number of contract-quality Herez as well as semi-old Herez in large sizes, but they have become a scarce article during the past few years. Again, I attribute this to the demand by Europe and the fact that the natives do not use many carpets larger than 10×14 ft. So it is natural that the supply of extra large-size Herez to America has been reduced by 80 percent. This could change some day, especially if there should be a recession in Europe.

I have wandered far afield from strict classification. We could make scores of classifications, such as floral designs or geometric designs.

GEOMETRIC DESIGN CARPETS

When one wants a geometric design carpet, approximately 9×12 ft. or larger, there are only the following:

Herez and Gorevans from Iran.

Mishkins and Ardabils from Iran. These Mishkins have seldom come as large as 9×12 ft. Sizes are usually 8×11 ft. and smaller. That can change, and may, but so far they do not have wider looms.

An Afshar Shiraz (good numbers about 8×11 ft., but only a very few as large as 9×12 ft.).

The Bokharas from Pakistan, which are strictly geometric.

The Afghans from Afghanistan.

Some few of the coarse Bahktiari carpets approach the geometric effect.

Only other rugs in carpet sizes in geometric designs are some of the light-colored rugs from India, principally those in the Chinese designs under many trade names. Our own trade name for one Chinese design is Keenlung.

LIGHT OR DARK COLORS

We can also make a classification according to light or dark colors. One of the problems of the rug dealer and salesman every day is presented by customers who have never bought an oriental rug coming in and indicating that they want a light-colored rug. Often they want the design to be soft and pastel.

They are quickly told that the softest of the Persian (Iranian) rugs are the Kirmans, one of the most expensive of all rugs. The Kirmans have a light creamy ivory or light champagne field. These rugs are lightly bleached after they arrive in America to give them the pastel and silky tone. Some come with backgrounds of pastel blue, or pastel green or rose.

Lately some few fine Kashans are being made in light colors and soft shades. Cost is about the same as the Kirman. Their fields are much more densely covered than most of the Kirmans, and most of these have the allover old Ispahan designs.

The third Persian rug in light colors and in the same general design as the Kirmans, is the Kasvin, a very heavy rug of good, average, tight weave and with good wool. This has been a favorite of ours because the price is so much less than the Kirman, and we believe it will last longer than any one lifetime. The design in these Kasvins will, as a rule, not be as pastel as that in the Kirman. Some few are. Again, the Kirman has had the light bleaching to obtain the pastel shades and the Kasvin has not.

The only other light-colored rugs with pastel shades are the orientals from India. The supply of these is large. As a class they are very beautiful and inexpensive compared to the higher priced Kirman and Kashan. To most people they are decorative and as beautiful as the Kirman, and we have many customers that actually like them better.

Other light-colored Persian rugs are the Kaputarhang, the Ramishan, and the Guenstepeh—all very much alike in general effect, but the Guenstepeh very much superior in quality and looks. But here the floral designs on the light field are quite colorful and not in the pastel shades.

Two other possibilities are the BOKHARAS FROM PAKISTAN that happen to come with the creamy ivory field. The Karachi quality, in addition to being finely woven, has a good nap and soft colors. The LaHore quality Bokhara will be found with the ivory field in limited numbers. The designs are not as soft but they have good colors.

CLASSIFICATION AS COLLECTORS' ITEMS

I have read much exaggeration in recent years in connection with many used rug sales when they list a whole column of rugs as being

Plate 39, above. ANTIQUE PRAYER DAGHESTAN from Caucasia. This is in the same general design as every one of these in museums throughout the world. Being in top condition, it is one of the choicest and finest rugs of this type in existence. Never to be found in the average estate, but only in a collection assembled forty to seventy-five years ago. Size 3.9 × 4.5 feet. *(Courtesy of Mr. and Mrs. J. Ogden Tyledsley, Jr., Cazenovia, New York). Plate 40, next page, on left.* ANTIQUE TALISH from Caucasia. The design is typical of every Talish rug —a rare type of Caucasian. The main border shown here is used invariably in all Talish rugs. This ancient rug is not in top condition. Because of its condition and its radical changes of color, most laymen would not buy a new oriental or

an ordinary old rug of this sort, but to a collector such radical changes of color in the open field of an antique rug would not be objectionable, but rather preferred. Size 3.5 × 7.6 feet. *(Courtesy of Mr. and Mrs. J. Ogden Tyldsley, Jr., Cazenovia, New York) Plate 41, above right.* ANTIQUE KUBA from Caucasia. A German writer has classed this as a Zejwa of the Kuba family. The large effulgent stars or coats-of-arms design is beautifully woven in many colors. The border design is referred to as Georgian or running dog. A perfect example of this type is the delight of every European buyer; even a thin one is in great demand. Size 11.4 × 4.3 feet. *(Courtesy of Mr. and Mrs. J. Ogden Tyldsley, Jr., Cazenovia, New York)*

189

collectors' items. Some 20 of the rugs listed will be nearly new Beloo-chistans, and maybe some 15 will be Ardabil rugs, which have only been made in the last 25 years. I have never seen one of these Ardabils that a real collector would consider to be a collectors' rug.

IT ALL DEPENDS ON HOW BROAD YOU WANT TO STRETCH THE TERM "COLLECTORS' ITEM OR RUG."

All my life I have believed, and told hundreds of collectors, that a rug, to be so classed, has to be one of the choicest examples of its type ever to be made. Just being an excellent rug is not sufficient. It has to be an art piece and as a rule it has to be antique or, at least, semi-antique. It must be a superb example of the type.

NOW, EVIDENTLY THE "COLLECTOR ITEM" TO MANY OF THESE DEALERS WHO LIST THEM IN USED RUG SALES, SIMPLY MEANS ANY SEMI-OLD RUG OF THE TYPE, AND PERHAPS THEIR DEFINITION OF "COLLEC-TION" IS A NUMBER OF DIFFERENT TYPES OF RUGS REGARDLESS OF TYPE, AGE, OR NAME.

Below are listed most of the names of the rugs that the collectors of the past 75 years have sought. Again, not just names but superb examples of each of the type.

These would all be scatter-size rugs, perhaps three or four of them runners, such as Talish from Caucasia, which was woven only in runner sizes.

Famous names like Herat, Polonaise, Ispahan, and other large-size rugs would not be included. Only the person of great wealth or a museum would think of collecting large rugs in these categories. First, they will not have the room to lay them out or show them from time to time, because they will never have enough floor space to use all their rugs, and besides it would be wrong to walk on many of these. They must be preserved as objects of art which will never again be produced. Perhaps many of the paintings of today will be masterpieces in the years to come, but there are thousands of good artists. With oriental rugs certain types have not been made for many years and never again can be woven.

Many good friends have asked me if I would make up a list of the rarest types that should go in a collection. So, here is a good list. A few others could be added. All are antique rugs, except the Nain and Qum.

From Iran	From Turkey*	From Caucasia*
Sena	Prayer Ghiordes	Prayer Daghestan
Feraghan	Prayer Kula	Kabistan
LaVer Kirman	Prayer Ladik	Kuba
Shiraz	Prayer Kum Kuppa	Shirvan
Niris	Hereke	Chichi
Kashan	Konia	Baku
Sarouk	Oushak**	Kazak
Joshigan	Melez	Geunge
Bijar	Prayer Melez	Karabaugh
Bijar Sampler	Bergamo	Tcherkess (Kazak)
Bahktiari	Kershehr	Talish
Veramin	Makri	
Nain	Dirmirdji	
Qum	Yuruk	
Suj-Bulak		

   * All woven before World War I.

   ** Only the rarest of small Oushaks. Many ordinary, cheap-grade Oushak carpets are being sold as rare Oushaks.

We have included Nain, finer than any of the other rugs listed here (with the exception possibly of Prayer Kum Kuppa and Hereke). Every collector will want one of these fine Nains regardless of it being new, and I would also add one of the best of the new Qums.

From Central Asia or the Bokhara Family

The best of the following in antique and choicest quality.
Pinde Bokhara
Salor Bokhara (rug or tent bag)
Tekke (or Royal Bokhara) (rug or tent bag)
Prayer Tekke (or Princess Bokhara)
Beshire
Yomud Tent Bag
Ersari Tent Bag
Afghan Bokhara (rug or tent bag)
Khiva Bokhara (small or larger size)

Finally, the MOST IMPORTANT CLASSIFICATION takes into

consideration the fact that rugs by the same name *vary greatly*. Do not, for one minute, get the idea that every rug in one of the above names is a collector's item. There are superior rugs by the name, there are average good rugs, and they are very poor rugs of the type in nearly every name rug. This classification is learned only through experience —handling rugs, seeing lots of rugs, and having lived with some good rugs.

RESUME

I had thoughts of writing or making a lengthy recapitulation, but I would only be repeating the many cautions and checks contained in the preceding chapters. Lest I sound too critical about all phases, I wish to repeat that the regular importing houses in New York are most reliable and their prices will vary, one from the other, very little. If the retailer based his selling price on a percentage based on these wholesale prices, we would have a good established price system. Unfortunately, we have a good number like the case we cited in Chapter Ten under "Highway Robbery," where a store advertised 2×3 Hamadan rugs regular $50.00 on sale for $24.95. And, unfortunately, there are some of the small jobbers in New York who will camouflage many defects— motheaten places, painting in worn areas—and putting them on used rug sales at ridiculous prices.

If I have alarmed you with all the many check points and warnings it is well, because it is a definite fact that a good percentage of all the rugs imported have some bad faults. Rugs with small to bad faults are not necessarily to be rejected, provided the price is right and you are looking for the so-called "bargain." I have always found that you can sell a rug with faults more quickly if you point them out to the customer, and not try to whitewash them with such statements as, "That makes the rug more oriental."

The greatest danger, as we have pointed out, lies in buying from a source from which you have no recourse once you have paid for the rug. So, if you stay away from itinerant auction sales, and from the professional used rug sales, and from the itinerant salesman that comes to town, even though he goes to a big store and sells through that store, you should have little trouble finding a good new rug at the right price. A difference between $10.00 to $25.00 on a small rug and $50.00 to $100.00 on a large rug that is the right rug, will be of little consequence in time.

So, once again, go to a regular rug dealer—the man who has been

Plate 42. ANTIQUE TABRIZ from Iran. A rare antique Tabriz with the field in burnt almond. This excellent example is valuable as a collector's item, but the rug's worth is diminished because of worn and neglected ends. No way to restore this. In buying such a rug a collector must leave it in this condition. The person who buys it for utility purpose must be prepared to spend thirty dollars or more to remove the narrow border all the way around, or to having one border missing at the ends. This detracts from the value.

in business for a good many years and who, you have reason to believe, will stand back of his rugs—and the chances are your rug will be good for a lifetime and will have some value for many years. At least 99 out of 100 of the people who buy from reliable sources will eliminate most of the element of gamble.

When it comes to buying a used rug, I believe that our detailed chapter can prove invaluable to the beginner, and even to the experienced rug buyer. Here, beyond any question, the risk is great. Again, if you know rugs, you are pretty safe anywhere. But my check list will help even the expert, and my top assistants as well.

I REPEAT—buy your used rug from the permanent dealer and not from one of the big used rug sales which these stores have used as a gimmick for volume.

The main warning I wish to issue in this Resume is to not be misled by the many magazine articles that have appeared in the last two or three months in a dozen magazines. There have been recent articles on the front page of the conservative *Wall Street Journal,* and in *Town & Country* magazine, *Newsweek, Reader's Digest,* and *Antiques Magazine,* just to mention a few of them. The principal theme of all of these articles is that antique rugs are an INVESTMENT.

Frankly, I am afraid that this kind of talk is going to influence many people to buy most any old rug that is called antique, and believe they have an investment in a work of art.

I and all the dealers throughout the country are grateful for these articles, whether they are good or bad, because they stimulate the business tremendously. Every importing house welcomes them regardless of whether the facts in the articles are right or not. From a sales point of view I, too, could be happy over these, but I have too many years behind me to think only of the few dollars, especially when so many hundreds of people send me requests for information believing that I can be relied on to make an unbiased opinion. The old slogan, "A little knowledge is a dangerous thing," could apply to most of these articles.

The fine article in the *Wall Street Journal* can be attributed to one of my customers who bought some rare rugs to hang in his office. He actually bought them for an investment and relied on us, but be sure we never told him that he would make money on these rare rugs. The trend for rare rugs, and the European demand for them from America as the only source of these rare rugs, have justified his hopes of investment.

Plate 43, upper left. ANTIQUE MUS-TAPHI FERAGHAN from Iran. A collector's item—will never be found in a used rug sale. Size 4.1 × 6.5 feet. *Plate 44, upper right.* ANTIQUE FERAGHAN from Iran. A real collector's item. Available from time to time—but usually worn out and not like this fine, lovely specimen. You will never find such a rug on the so-called "collector's list" of a used rug sale. Size 4.2 × 6.5 feet. *Plate 45, right.* ANTIQUE SENNA from Iran. A collector's item seldom seen even in an estate sale today. Size 4.4 × 6.6 feet. *(Plates 43–45 courtesy of Prof. Robert Fisher, Blacksburg, Va.)*

195

Plate 46, left. ANTIQUE SENNA from Iran. Rare, old Senna with the floriated pear design in the field and a most unusual and exquisite border for a Senna. This is not the typical design found in the Senna, but one of the best known Persian designs. A rare piece of museum quality. Old Sennas of any type have not been imported since about 1924. Size 7.5 × 4.6 feet. *Plate 47, right.* ANTIQUE ZELI-SULTAN from Iran. The small Feraghan or Herati design is used almost invariably in these rugs. Field may be either blue or red— usually a fairly bright red even when very old. This one is blue. None of these have been imported since about 1928. A good example is invaluable. Practially all are finely woven and valuable, though more than half of them have the defect of bleeding colors. This is one of the perfect ones. Size 6.5 × 4 feet. *(Plates 46 and 47 courtesy of Mr. and Mrs. Joseph H. King, Jr., Syracuse, New York).*

196

Plate 48, above. ANTIQUE PRAYER MELEZ from Turkey. Invariably will have tawny burnt almond shades in the field and border. The conventionalized turtle design in the border is almost always in lavender or deep plum. The shadings or changes of color in the field are unimportant and do not detract from the collector's evaluation. Size 5.8 × 4.3 feet. *Plate 49, right.* ANTIQUE MAKRI from Turkey. A rare type of rug not to be found in many collections, even when thin. Size 4 × 2.8 feet. This and the rug above are among the rare old Turkish types not made since the turn of the century. *(Courtesy of Mr. and Mrs. Joseph H. King, Jr., Syracuse, New York)*

197

Frankly speaking, I do not advise anyone to buy as an investment rare rugs at the prices they command today. I believe most of the Caucasian rugs are already overpriced, and it will take a good many years for them to catch up with the scarcity and rarity point of view.

Down through my 46 years in the business, and I am speaking of up until about 1960, customers used to say to me, "Do you think these rugs are a good investment?" We never once sold that idea. I recall lawyers for estates saying to me that the rugs were the first to sell and sold for more than had originally been paid for them. And they would ask, "Oriental rugs are really a good investment, aren't they?" Invariably my reply was that I would not say an investment, but I would say that a good rug was always worth money and that over the years they were the least expensive floor covering of any type of rug every conceived. When it came to the rugs that were rare, and I mean real collector's items that were rare in 1920, and not by any means the types advertised in used rug sales as "collector's items," I felt and probably said that they would always be worth good money and probably more, from time to time, due to rarity. The people who bought these rare rugs generally bought them as collector's items and as lovers of the great art that rare oriental rugs make up. I know of only one case where a collector bought them with the idea of investment and as a hedge against inflation. My great friend still lives in Seneca Falls, New York, and knows that he could make a large profit off his rugs, but he is too much in love with them to sell them even at his 85 years of age.

For you to buy a rare rug—and by rare I mean a rug a collector has owned for 40 years and his estate now puts back on the market—these particular items which can never be produced again, always bring big prices. They will be worth whatever one is willing to pay for them. I fear that the Germans and other European buyers have already overpaid for these. The New York jobber has been a good salesman and, in fact, a "gouger" in many of these sales. It is my opinion that most knowledgeable American collectors and dealers are not going to agree with these prices. The first time that there is any trouble in the economy in Europe, these prices are not going to be maintained.

So, what I am saying is that with all these magazines talking about "investment" I cannot go along with them anymore than I believe in buying stocks when they are at an all time high—yet a lot of people do buy these stocks and rugs, and maybe they will be right.

Now, what chance have you got of getting a rare Ladik, Melez,

Plate 50. ANTIQUE PRAYER GHIORDES from Turkey. Probably early 18th century. Rarest and most valuable of Turkish (Anatolian) prayer rugs. Type was rare in 1900. While somewhat worn, the rug is still valuable and a collector's item. Any collector is glad to get even a worn one, but the better the condition the more valuable it is. If you think you have found one, check with an expert to make sure it is not one of the cheap editions appearing in the 1915–1930 period. Difference is unmistakable, but beginners can be badly fooled.

Feraghan and the others listed, at a bargain price? Absolutely none! The trouble with these magazine articles is that they are going to encourage a lot of people to think that any old antique rug they pick up at a used rug sale is an investment. Many of these bring high inflated prices when they are not worth half the amount, and if these old, thin rugs, many of which have had the background touched up, are put in the hall or living room and used for 10 to 15 years more, they are going to be beyond repair and of no value whatsoever. Not one in a thousand of these, of perhaps several thousand, are going to be the real rare type that in a worn condition a curator in a museum would accept.

During the past 60 years people have been buying chemically washed and painted rugs—Sarouks and the like—thinking they would last a lifetime, and maybe someone sold them the investment idea. The belief that any chemically washed and painted rug could ever be an investment has now been completely debunked. The only chance of your oriental rug becoming more valuable lies in buying a good average type, not the rarest antique and semi-antique, and especially a good new rug. If you buy an antique or semi-antique Hamadan, or Ingelas, or Kashan, or any one of many types, and give them average good care, it should be in pretty good condition 25 to 40 years from now. And with continued gradual inflation and increased scarcity, these rugs no doubt will be worth more money in time. And the chances are also good that any fine new rug from Persia or Pakistan will increase greatly in value.

With the present determination by the Shah of Iran to increase sharply the standard of living of the rug weavers, it seems logical that new rugs will cost a little more each year—probably a lot more. Some types will practically disappear from the market simply because the weavers will get several times as much salary in a factory. Many new factories are being built in the large cities everywhere. So, the city rugs, or those woven in the large weaving plants, will be the hardest hit. Those woven out in the country where there are no factories, should not go up as much. Any good Persian rug is going to be good property—it is going to cost you less than any other floor covering over the years— and it is going to be less effort to care for.

Now, if I were going to name an investment rug, one of the finest NAINS, with some 600 knots to the square inch, seems to me to have a better chance of becoming a good investment than most of the rare antique rugs. In no period in the last 400 years in Persia has a group of rugs come out so finely woven and so exquisite as these are. Some few

Plate 51. ANTIQUE YURUK from Turkey. A type no longer imported—not woven since prior to World War I. However, it never obtained collector's status to the extent that most other Turkish rugs did. This type is almost always very crooked—being woven out in the country on poor looms. The irregularity in shape would be objectionable to almost anyone except the rabid collector.

others are close to them. And if I were going to recommend rugs with possibilities, certainly I would not pass by the many wonderful Bokharas being woven in Pakistan. Here the uncertain Pakistani government could discontinue the subsidy on these rugs and they would go up overnight. I would also think that one of the new Mishkin rugs from Northern Iran in the likeness of the old Caucasian rugs would, in years, prove a better buy than one of the old thin Caucasian rugs that are so overpriced today.

Finally, remember that a rug, in order to become more valuable, requires some time to elapse to become scarce and for the inflation to have continued. Of course, anyone who bought a good oriental rug in the 1930 period can sell that rug, assuming it is in good condition, for much more than he paid for it. So is everything else higher. I most certainly would like to agree with all these magazine articles which are, for the most part, listing a few rugs that are seldom to be had today and leading the public to the belief that any antique rug is an investment. I agree that those mentioned have proven to be such, but at today's prices the buyer may have a long wait for his high-priced rug to make him a profit. I would not advise anyone to buy rugs for investment. Buy them as collector's items—buy them for beautiful floor covering. Have the thought in mind, if you wish, that in years to come they will be worth more perhaps than any other article you use in the home.

I like to think of people buying oriental rugs because they are so delightful to live with; I like to think of the old banker, the greatest Scrooge I ever met, in a little town near Syracuse. We used to sell his next door neighbor, a doctor, many rugs. Each time, in my young years, as I went there with rugs, the banker's wife would come over and then she would telephone her husband to ask if she could not try one of them. The answer was always "no." Finally, as years went by, he broke down and bought one, and eventually my people sold him rugs for every space in his home. He could not resist them, and when I came back from the last war his wife and daughter came to me and told me he had died, and I recall them telling me that the greatest pleasure he ever had in life, besides his family, were these rugs. And he would say to his family on a cold winter day with snow everywhere outside, "Look at the Spring. Don't these rugs bring Spring right into the living room? How could we have ever lived without them?" So, you will forgive me if I do not go along with the idea of buying rugs for an investment.

And I repeat that I think that these magazines, while helping the dealer, have done a great disservice to the general public, and thousands of people will buy a wornout antique or ordinary rug, and I am afraid too often pay too much, and have no investment—in fact, very little value for resale or trade.

Again, my parting advice is to repeat, "It is well to recognize first as last, the indisputable fact that you cannot now secure desirable oriental rugs for a song, and that it is safe to rest assured generally that he who sells an oriental rug very cheap, is selling a *very cheap* oriental rug as well."

INDEX

206